Your way is **STUPID**

Your Way Is Stupid!

There has to be a better way

A conversational Bible study by

JOHNSON

&

SORBE

(sore-bee)

XULON PRESS

Xulon Press
2301 Lucien Way #415
Maitland, FL 32751
407.339.4217
www.xulonpress.com

Illustrated by Kia Andrews
Editors: Jessi Thompson & Heather Hagness

Paperback ISBN-13: 978-1-6628-5395-1
Hard Cover ISBN-13: 978-1-6628-5396-8
Ebook ISBN-13: 978-1-6628-5397-5

Dedication

Johnson

SOLI DEO GLORIA
"He only is my Rock and my Salvation; He is my Defense and my Fortress, I shall not be moved. With God rests my salvation and my glory; He is my Rock of unyielding strength and impenetrable hardness, and my refuge is in God!"
Psalm 62:5-7 (AMPC)

Sorbe

To Brian, August, & Owen; I dedicate this first official written work to you.

Table of Contents

Hi Reader!

We are so glad you bought our book, and we want you to get the most benefit out of it! You know how you buy a certain brand of shampoo, and they want you to buy their conditioner and gel, too, for the fullest and most glorious locks of hair possible? Think about our suggestions that way. This study, if read and applied, will produce positive life changing results. Here are a couple of our recommendations as you get started.

1. Go through this book with a friend
2. Use it as a group book study

As you practice being OPEN, you will begin to see God show up in miraculous and tangible ways. You will find encouragement from hearing and sharing what God is doing in your life and the lives of your friends.

Foreword

Tony

Some of you might find some humor in this title. Others might find it downright offensive. Who do these women think they are to tell you your way is stupid? We might be ashamed to admit it, but sometimes we think our way is pretty darn clever. We live in a society that worships the self-made man or woman who beats the odds and overcomes adversity. Years ago, the famous singer Frank Sinatra summed up the overarching worldview with his lyrics: "I did it my way." After all, isn't it my way or the highway? Is there any other way?

Joe

This book could have easily been called "My Way is Stupid" and it would have been fitting to the text, as we find Johnson and Sorbe are very open and honest about all the ways they have fallen short of the glory of God. It's a serious notion that we can see God in our midst today or we can miss God amidst the noise, fear, and insecurity within our hearts.

Tony

Johnson and Sorbe are two women I have known for quite some time. When I was 14, I moved to a small town named

Jackson, Minnesota. Up until that point, I had lived in one of the largest suburbs of Minneapolis–a city named Bloomington. When I moved to Jackson, a small town of about 3,500 people, I wasn't exactly sure what adventures God had in store. I started volunteering with Johnson at the local nursing home, giving weekly devotional messages to the residents. We worked together on a regular basis, and I was able to learn from her. I also got to know Sorbe as a youth leader in our youth group. It has been encouraging to see them grow and share what they have learned over the years in this book!

Joe

My relationship with both Jen and Jenn may seem a bit abstract. I have known Jennifer Johnson for the better part of ten years, meeting through her magnificent, studly husband. I was working as a community outreach director on the Pine Ridge Indian reservation. He was a youth pastor and had brought his students to my "Rez". We began to connect immediately, so much so that even today I would call Mark my spiritual twin. I emphasize spiritual... he is a tall, white, good looking athletic guy; whilst I am a short Middle Eastern obese fellow. We look nothing close to family, but I have met few people who understand me as well as Mark. Often, when my wife (Nicole) and I would visit her hometown in Wisconsin, the Johnson residence would be our midway check point. It was there I met Jenny and learned about her heart, realizing within minutes that my buddy Mark had found someone equally as amazing. Jenn Sorbe I met through my current church in southern Wisconsin. We were a small multi-campus church, and I was serving as a youth pastor at our Jefferson campus at the time. My mind was blown after discovering she had worked with Mark and Jenny in Jackson–such a small world! I was not aware of all the God moments these two ladies would bring into my life in our, honestly, very limited interactions. I am so grateful for the two of them and I know they have given all they have to the Lord for this book!

Tony

Read this book! The three sections speak to important parts of the Christian walk. When we open ourselves to God, trust the process and have no fear–we begin to walk in the life Christ intends for us! Jesus reminds us in the book of John that He came so we can have life and life to the full. This life is not found through stubbornly insisting on our own way. The "have it your way" life only works at Burger King and isn't a good approach to life at all. Johnson and Sorbe will remind you that perhaps there is a better way. Some of you need to hear this shouted. But some of you already know deep down that your way is stupid and there must be a better way. Thankfully, this is where our God loves to meet us. He loves to meet us in our desperation when our backs are against the wall.

As you dive into this book, I encourage you to read with an open mind. Ask questions. Write down your thoughts. Discuss this book with people around you. Pray. Seek the Lord and He will reveal Himself. American culture (and cultures all over the world) are hurting right now and looking for a better hope, especially in light of the global health pandemic and seeming chaos wherever we turn. Perhaps there is a better way to be found in Jesus. And yes, perhaps it begins with the admission that your way is stupid, after all!

Joe

Reading this book led me to pause countless times, challenging me in new ways. I have always understood a certain level of surrender to the Lord; but I underestimated the small, simple, necessary, and incredibly impactful ways we can be fully submerged in His presence when we walk in complete obedience. This "stupid" book has challenged the very roots of my faith. I know without a doubt that I am not alone. The Church needs to be brought back to a simple place of surrender before the Lord. Even if you've heard the message before, it is important to hear it again and again from multiple angles and depths. God has personally guided this book. He has led these women through heart transformation, and I guarantee it can be the catalyst point of authentic surrender to the call of Jesus and the heart of the father, like it was for me, if you allow it. I pray that as you read this book, you will open your hands and trust the process of what God is speaking to you and walk in the faith that casts out fear; because you will learn how to accomplish all those purposes with this book if you let the spirit teach you through these authors.

INTRODUCING STUPID

"Whoever trusts in his own mind is a fool, but he who walks in wisdom will be delivered."
Proverbs 28:26 (ESV)

"Now the trouble about trying to make yourself stupider than you really are is that you very often succeed."
C.S. Lewis, The Magician's Nephew

"Stupid is as stupid does."
Forrest Gump

Johnson

We all have our own special kind of stupid. Everyone does. It starts when we are young, often becoming blatantly obvious in our teenage years, and develops into a comfortable routine in adulthood. Stupid will feel like a harsh or tame word, depending on your background. Whether you perceive the word in a positive or negative light, our way of doing things is ultimately stupid in comparison to God's way of doing things. Sorbe and I did not love this word at first. We debated over the use of it in the title. Our initial concern over the controversial nature of the word stupid has morphed into a deep appreciation. It sets the tone for the whole book by contrasting the stupidity of our own small-minded mistakes to God's perfect will for us. I really do love that God is vastly bigger and more intelligent than me! It is much easier to trust His plans for my life...even when His way seems stupid.

As a child, teenager, and then young adult, I felt vastly superior to many people in the Bible. Moses? What a gigantic man-baby with a lack of temper control. First, he killed a man in a moment of rage. Then, when God asked him to be His mouthpiece, he shirked his duties and passed the responsibility of speaking to his brother. Eventually, out of anger, he struck a rock twice in disobedience, ultimately leading to his inability to enter the promised land. Women in the Bible are equally guilty of stupidity. Eve ate the forbidden fruit, Sarah (Abraham's wife) set her husband up with another woman, and Lot's wife disobeyed God and was turned into a pillar of salt...

Let's pause here. Take your time and enjoy this moment. Think about all the people in the Bible who messed up. Feel free to point a very serious finger of judgment.

Now I want you to point that finger over here while Sorbe and I share our own battles with stupidity. In this book we will dig into some personal and Biblical examples of stupid. Then, we will transition into a discussion on how God changed our lives through practicing the Biblical principles of *open, trust the process,* and *no fear*. Together, we are about to walk a very important road. Now would be a great time for you to find a notebook or a piece of paper, or simply a pen to write in the margins of this book. I know that God will bring things to your mind as we share; He will gently reveal past and present areas of spiritual weakness in your life. He intends to do surgery on each of us.

Proverbs 28:26 reads, "Whoever trusts in his own mind is a fool, but he who walks in wisdom will be delivered." The wisdom that comes from God leads to deliverance. This is our prayer for you. We pray, as you seek the Lord, that He will remove every chain keeping you from experiencing true freedom in Christ. A wise and dear friend, a feisty elderly woman named Ethel, once said, "If a pastor doesn't kick you in the pants once in a while, he isn't worth having." Ethel didn't want to waste her remaining years on this Earth doing nothing—she expected growth and change.

Sorbe

Prepare to have your pants kicked!

1–GOD'S WAY SEEMS STUPID

"And one standing alone can be attacked and defeated, but two can stand back-to-back and conquer; three is even better, for a triple-braided cord is not easily broken."
Ecclesiastes 4:12 (TLB)

"My heart is breaking, in a way I never thought it could. My mind is racing, With the question, 'Are you still good?' Can you make something, From the wreckage? Would you take this heart, And make it whole again? Though the mountains may be moved into the sea, though the ground beneath might crumble and give way, I can hear my Father singing over me, "It's gonna be OK, it's gonna be OK."
Tasha Layton, "Into the Sea (It's Gonna Be Ok)"

Johnson

Giving up control isn't easy. It is a process. It reminds me of a child who gets a shard of glass stuck in his palm. His mother stands above him, ready with the tweezers. The child, in fear of the pain, clenches his fist protectively guarding the piece of glass. He protects the very thing that wounded him in the first place. With constant reassuring words, his mother coaxes him to open his hand. Reluctantly, the child opens his fist, and the glass is finally removed. God is a good Father who holds my hands, reassuring me that I can trust Him.

As the wife of a husband in ministry, the mother of five girls (pregnant with our sixth child), and a recent move behind us–my "normal" was already more than a full-time job. Things were crazy, but my constant stream of adrenaline kept me *feeling* in control. My mother-in-law was all set to watch our kids and I climbed into the minivan with my towering 6'9" husband. We were finally off and on our way to Minneapolis for Mark's surgery. This was the second operation on his knee since tearing his PCL while playing football at youth group. More than a year of regular medical appointments and physical therapy left me feeling prepared for what was ahead of us. I wouldn't say I was excited about his surgery, but I was intent on being a solid support for my husband. We checked into our hotel, and as I struggled to go to sleep that night, my biggest fears revolved around the drive home. I remember worrying about how Mark would handle the hour-long drive after just having had surgery. I prayed that we would not hit rush hour, to ensure we would have a peaceful trip home.

We arrived early for Mark's appointment and his procedure went much better than expected. We felt optimistic as we left the hospital. It was well before rush hour, and we were excited to be making good time. *Wow! I'm in control. Everything is working out just as I planned.* The day would have been victorious had it ended here. Little did we know that a life altering event was about to occur.

After placing my dear, tall husband in the back seat of our minivan, we buckled up and headed for home. We entered road construction after driving less than a mile on the freeway. In a flash, someone ahead of us slammed on his brakes. I witnessed a ripple effect of cars braking and swerving to avoid hitting one another. I slammed on my brakes, barely avoiding a rear end collision. My heart was racing, pounding hard in my chest. I felt a momentary wave of satisfaction over successfully escaping an accident—and then we were struck hard from behind. I heard tires screeching and glass shattering. I was no longer in control. This was not part of the plan!

God's grace and protection was still in our midst. Just a mile back, on the same freeway, there "happened" to be an ambulance. Within minutes, a medic stood outside my window. Tapping on the glass, he snaps me out of my shocked state. "Ma'am, are you and your passenger alright?" Unable to emotionally connect with his question, my words tumble out. I state how my husband has just come out of surgery and I frantically struggle to put my thoughts and words together. I hear Mark ask from the back, "Is our baby okay?" I gasp. In the chaos and shock, I had completely forgotten about my baby. *I am pregnant.* Quickly assessing myself and my round belly, I feel okay. *Thank you, Lord,* I quietly breathe.

My baby and I were fine, but not Mark. During the crash, because of his height, his head slammed hard on the ceiling and his neck snapped backwards into the headrest. He was confused and in pain. He wasn't himself. *Could it be leftover anesthesia from his surgery or is something worse going on?* By the time the second ambulance arrived, the consensus was that Mark had sustained a concussion, though no one knew to what extent. Back to the hospital he went... only this time on a stretcher in an ambulance. That singular event would massively alter our lives in the most significant of ways. Day by day it became more and more evident that things were spiraling out of my control.

Mark's brain injury became an all-consuming battle, one that stole even our simplest dreams. Three months after the accident, I gave birth to our sixth child amidst the hardship. Mark was a youth pastor at our new church and was still committed to going into the office. However, because of the trauma to his brain, he found himself sitting in a dark office, alone, the majority of the time. He couldn't follow a conversation. Any work he did utterly drained him. His blood pressure was skyrocketing, and I was becoming more and more concerned. With six children at home, the constant commotion was overwhelming and gave his brain no rest from outside stimulation. The doctor advised Mark to stop working altogether, stating that if he continued, it would kill him. Mark needed total darkness and silence for an unspecified time if he was going to heal. Not only was he being told he had to stop working, he was ultimately being told he could no longer be around his family. To keep him alive, we had to let him go.

Mark loved being a Youth Pastor and he wasn't ready to give it up, but I was praying our church would release him. Not long after my prayer, we met with two church leaders to discuss Mark's health. Internally I wanted to beg my dear friends to fire my husband, but I found myself just sitting there not able to say a word. Tears welling up in my eyes, I was silently begging them to hear me. They had come to the meeting simply to offer help and encouragement. Before anyone realized what was being said, the question was posed, "Would it be best if we just let you go?" The words hung in the air. Our friends were crushed, but I was relieved. God was saving my husband. It was love that led them to this decision. My poor husband was moved into my grandmother's basement, alone and in the dark. I stepped in where he had to step out.

MY DESPERATION TURNED INTO A DESPERATE NEED FOR JESUS

In the months following the accident, I found myself functioning purely in survival mode. I didn't have time to process my emotions. Thinking beyond the minute in front of me felt impossible. I was running on a lack of sleep. The added responsibility of time-consuming paperwork and phone calls created extra responsibility. I sold or gave away two-thirds of our belongings in order to move back in with my parents. My kids were emotional. Everyone needed me. I began to realize that at any moment I could break.

Just one week after moving, I signed my children up for Vacation Bible School at my parent's church. I just wanted something normal. I cannot express how much I wanted my children to have some stability amidst all that we had going on. But we were no longer living a normal life. This fact became painfully obvious on the last day when I picked up my girls from VBS. I had arrived early and, as I parked, I looked back to see my infant son sleeping peacefully in his car seat. I took a few deep breaths, trying to stuff my grief deep inside. I sat in the car and closed my eyes to take a moment. Upon opening them, I looked at the clock and saw I was late. *Where did the time go?* I jumped from my seat and sprinted into the church. A lady inside looked at me and stated, "That's nice, you got someone to watch your baby." *Oh, NO!* I was THAT parent! I had just carelessly left my child in the car. Tears filled my eyes and I ran back to the van where my baby boy peacefully slept. I pulled him out of his car seat and held him close. I tried to remain sane as I rushed back into the church to retrieve my children.

I finally had my last child collected when her teacher stopped me. She kindly spoke, "Oh, your daughter was such a delight in class. I hear you just moved here. What brings you to this area? What does your husband do?" Her innocent questions broke me. I was not ready. I felt vulnerable and exposed; my tears flowed freely. My children wrapped themselves around me and this sweet teacher prayed over all of us. Though my hardship didn't end in that hallway, God has carried me through the last four years, healing me in ways I wasn't aware needed healing and shifting my perspective. My desperation turned into a desperate need for Jesus. I could no longer handle my life without Him. I needed Him to walk beside me and give me the strength to keep going.

How could this hardship be God's plan for my life? Unbeknownst to me, behind the scenes God was already calling in reinforcements to come alongside me through this time. He would also use my sweet children to teach me many powerful lessons. What I hadn't realized yet was that I was actually in a spiritual battle. It was war! However, I was unarmed and unaware. I was doing my best in my own power, yet God loved me too much to allow me to stay in that place. Ecclesiastes 4:9-10 says, "Two are better than one, because they have a good reward for their toil. For if they fall, one will lift up his fellow. But woe to him who is alone when he falls and has not another to lift him up!"

> *"You've kept track of my every toss and turn through the sleepless nights, Each tear entered in your ledger, each ache written in your book."*
>
> Psalm 56:8 (MSG)

HE WAS COLLECTING HER TEARS IN HIS LEDGER, WORKING BEHIND THE SCENES THE WHOLE TIME.

Sorbe

God heard Johnson's cries for help. He was collecting her tears in His ledger, working behind the scenes the whole time. In Deuteronomy 31:6, God states He never leaves us or turns His back on us. He saw her. And you know what? He found Johnson a buddy to do battle with. Someone who would step into a call neither of them expected. God had plans to do a mighty work in both their lives–far greater than the lives they had once lived.

Who did God call? He called me.

Johnson and I knew each other from a small Minnesota town we had both lived in. I volunteered as a youth leader with her husband who was the youth pastor. We did a few functions together, mostly within the confines of church outreach. My family ended up moving to Wisconsin about the same time that Johnson's family moved north. We lost track of each other as I invested in a new place and a new life. Johnson's life–well, you can see why she lost track of me. I was just doing life. Nothing special. Nothing profound. Life was good. But God was going to call on me in an unusual way. A dream. Two dreams in fact. I have had only a handful of what I would call spiritual dreams in my lifetime. They are the ones you wake up from and you can't shake.

My first dream: I found myself in a dark room. I was on a low stage, seated in a chair and holding a baby. I knew I was holding

Johnson's new infant, though in waking life, I had never met him. To my right, two narrow steps down from me, also seated in a chair, was Johnson's husband, Mark. The room was dark, except the space where he and I were sitting. He was staring at me, unblinkingly. I could not read his expression. I looked down at the infant and back up at Mark's focused gaze. The mood was indistinct, no urgency, no fear, just a question: *What am I doing here and why is Mark staring at me*? There was no fear or anxiety or inappropriateness to it. Just intent, staring at my face, into my eyes. He did not move or blink. Again, I looked down at the infant in my arms and then at Mark, down at the infant and then at Mark. I wondered what he wanted and then I woke up.

Once awake, I could not shake the dream from my mind. I shared it with my husband and he suggested I give them a call. Subsequently I decided to put the curious dream behind me and moved on with my day. Two nights later, I had a similar dream. This time it seemed as if Mark hijacked it. One moment I was swimming in an underwater city with my two sons and the next moment I was inside a dark, indistinct concrete room. The room was unremarkable; the only lit area was where I was standing. There again, standing to my right, was Mark, staring intently without expression. I woke up. Though I was perplexed by the "why" behind these unusual dreams, I did feel it was a message to call them, one I could no longer ignore.

Ring, ring.

I didn't even have the chance to say hello. Johnson answered the phone with, "Thank God, you called!" I had little opportunity to speak as she updated me on their life of brokenness, heartache, and sorrow. She began telling me about Mark's accident and subsequent brain injury. She told me how broken and hurt Mark was because of it. He had lost the very job they moved up north to do. A position he felt God had created for him and now he was incapacitated and placed in a basement to "heal." Mark was now recovering away from his family, and Johnson was caring for them all. Though she was *not* alone, in many ways she *felt* very alone. At that time, she was breastfeeding their infant who additionally did not sleep well through the night. She was caring for their five young girls who in their own ways were each hurting and grieving the loss of their father, afraid that he would never fully recover from his injury. She questioned how they would survive all this. She was homeschooling, cooking, cleaning, and now taking on the responsibilities Mark used to do. It was hard for her to make it through each day. Johnson was an empty vessel in survival mode, giving all of herself to her children, scarcely holding on to her own sanity. She was desperately grasping the fact that God is a good God, but secretly wondering how *good* He really was because her life was in a world of hurt and confusion. She was beaten down, broken, and desperate for another type of salvation, one that would save her from the nightmare she was in.

I was stunned. Deep down, I knew God had called me to be a battle buddy for Mark and Johnson, but at the time I had no idea what the call meant or how to fight. So I did the only thing I knew to do–I cried like a baby after I hung up the phone and I prayed for God's guidance!

The reality was the Lord saw her pain and He was calling in reinforcements. I was one of them and Johnson would not have to walk through that season alone. Using those two dreams, the Holy Spirit called me to be a prayer warrior for a friend in need; and, as a result, He would launch a ministry between two unlikely people. If any of you think that God is no longer talking to us, it's time to start actively listening again. The world and beyond are far bigger than any of us can Imagine.

Let me be vulnerable and up front with you right now. I did not feel worthy to be called into this position. I knew a basic, one-and-done "I pray it all gets better" prayer, along with a grocery gift card was not going to be enough. The stuff she was facing was heavy and she was facing it daily. It wasn't just going to go away. Johnson needed a true prayer warrior, an intercessor, whatever that was. I had heard the word intercessor before and knew it was the term for someone who was really good at praying powerfully, but I was pretty sure that was not me.

"God," I cried out, "you have the wrong person! I have no idea how to pray powerfully enough to see Mark healed. How can I help Jenny raise her kids when she lives in another state? Her life is awful, God! My life is good. I can't even relate to her situation. That's not fair to her! How can I be the one you called?!" (I am crying even as I write this in the book. I now have the blessing of looking back on the last four years and seeing all that God has done to change my prayer life and how Johnson really did need me to step in. I am so very glad I listened.) In that tearful moment, God allowed me to cry and speak out all my fears. I asked Him out loud, "*How* can I do this thing you've asked me to do God? I don't even know how to do what you've asked." He answered me right away in my mind.

I EXPECTED TO HEAR FROM HIM.
I WAS DESPERATE AND I WAS
LISTENING FOR THE ANSWER.

You see, God knows me intimately. He knows how I think and what I need to hear. He knows you, too, by the way. And guess what? I expected to hear from Him. I was desperate and I was listening for the answer. If He was calling me, then He would lead me. At the moment of my desperate prayer, I heard a familiar statement, "Then do something about it." His answer was familiar because someone had said it to me before and it was a call to action. As soon as I heard that familiar statement, my tears stopped. I wiped my face, stood up, and said, "Okay then, I will learn. Jenny needs me and You called me. Time to suck it up and drive on. I'm in, God. You lead and I will follow."

The first thing I needed to do was carve time into my life specifically for God. Even though I had spent 12 years in the military, I had become a night owl and I was no longer as scheduled as I once was. So, I watched two YouTubes on how to wake up early and be successful. You may laugh at this, but it actually helped me. I spoke to my husband and let him know that I would be waking up early to read and learn; he was welcome to join me, but I would no longer be staying up late. Within a week from that call, I was setting my alarm and getting up at 5:30am to sit with God for an hour.

And so it began for me; and, ultimately, for Johnson and Mark as well. I had a new purpose and a drive. I agreed to God's plan. I was unaware of the growth and freedom that was going to come from stepping into this seeking role. I needed answers from God that applied towards Jenny's difficulties. I needed to know how to respond with powerful biblical truth and how to love on her broken heart. And little did I know that by waking up early to spend time with God, I was actually going to grow in more ways than I could even imagine. I started reading books about miracles, prayer, and spiritual warfare. Sometimes I just sat there quietly, listening to anything God might want to say. I was reading the Bible again with new excitement. Day after day, I woke up and spent time with God. I began to look forward to going to bed at night because I was so excited to wake up for my special time in the morning. It became my favorite part of the day and I was learning so much!

God called me when I felt unqualified. His plan seemed stupid. In Exodus 4:10-12, we see Moses struggling with the same self-esteem issues. "Then Moses said to the Lord, 'O my Lord, I am not eloquent, neither before nor since You have spoken to Your servant; but I am slow of speech and slow of tongue." So the Lord said to him, "Who has made man's mouth? Or who makes him mute, or deaf, or seeing, or blind? Have not I, the Lord? Now therefore, go, and I will be with your mouth and teach you what you shall say."

When I said yes to God's plan and to prayerfully fight for the Johnson family, I had no idea what I was signing up for. I thought I had my life figured out and I was in a good place. I didn't realize all I had been missing out on spiritually. I started seeking God in ways I had not done before because God had a much better plan that would change my life, and my family's life, for the better. The battle was on, but we were about to see it for what it really was and how to be active soldiers in the war over our very lives. And not just soldiers, but conquerors.

> *"You, dear children, are from God and have overcome them, because the one who is in you is greater than the one who is in the world."*
>
> 1 John 4:4 (NIV)

> *"If God is for us, who can ever be against us?"*
>
> Romans 8:31b (NLT)

Group Discussion Questions/Action Step/ Personal Reflection/Journal:

- Johnson felt alone even though her parents took her in and she had her children with her. Have you ever felt alone even though you were not literally alone?

  If you feel comfortable, please share with your group what that was like for you.

- Sorbe cried when she got off the phone with Johnson. She felt unqualified for the position she knew Johnson needed filled.

  Share a time you stepped into something even though you felt unqualified.

Assignment: Step in for a friend. Here are some easy ideas to give you inspiration.

- Invite a friend to lunch
- Invite a friend to go on a hike/walk with you
- Send them an encouraging note in the mail/email/messenger
- Call a friend and ask them how they are doing. Ask them what they need prayer for. Go deeper by praying right there on the spot for anything they are having a hard time with.

"God doesn't call the qualified,
He qualifies the called."
Mark Batterson

Prayer:

Dear Jesus,

Help me to see and hear Your call for my life. I know there is more to this life than I am considering. I want You to teach me. I am sorry for going about life not realizing You want to teach me so much more. I desire to step into an active role of seeking You.

In Jesus' name I pray. Amen

2–GOD IS SMARTER

"This is because the foolishness of God is not foolishness at all and is wiser than men far beyond human comprehension, and the weakness of God is stronger than men far beyond the limits of human effort. Just look at your own calling, believers; not many of you were considered wise according to human standards, not many powerful or influential, not many of high and noble birth. But God has selected for His purpose the foolish things of the world to shame the wise revealing their ignorance, and God has selected for His purpose the weak things of the world to shame the things which are strong revealing their frailty."

1 Corinthians 1:25-27 (AMP)

"Such is man's nature, that he is very inactive and lazy unless he is influenced by some affection, either love or hatred, desire, hope, fear, or some other. These affections we see to be the springs that set men agoing, in all the affairs of life, and engage them in all their pursuits: these are the things that put men forward, and carry them along."

Jonathan Edwards, (Religious Affections)

Johnson

"God is smarter" may seem like an obvious statement. I feel most Christians, if asked, "Who is smarter...you or God?" would quickly answer, "God." But, knowing something and walking in that belief are two entirely different things. For example, one may feel recycling is important, but never personally recycle. This is the difference between memorizing a cookbook and actually using the knowledge to prepare, cook, and savor a delicious recipe. In this chapter, we are going to examine a story in the Bible of someone who thought his way was better, a man named Lot. Before we dig into this section, please read the following verses from Genesis 19.

> *"When morning dawned, the angels urged Lot [to hurry], saying, "Get up! Take your wife and two daughters who are here [and go], or you will be swept away in the punishment of the city." But Lot hesitated and lingered. The men took hold of his hand and the hand of his wife and the hands of his two daughters, because the Lord was merciful to him [for Abraham's sake]; and they brought him out, and left him outside the city [with his family]. When they had brought them outside, one [of the angels] said, "Escape for your life! Do not look behind you, or stop anywhere in the entire valley; escape to the mountains [of Moab], or you will be consumed and swept away." But Lot said to them, "Oh no, [not that place] my lords! Please listen, your servant has found favor in your sight, and you have magnified your loving kindness (mercy) to me by saving my life; but I cannot escape to the mountains, because the disaster will overtake me and I will be killed."*
>
> Genesis 19:15-19 (AMP)

Lot and his family are probably one of my favorite examples of living stupid. This man could easily make the top ten list of dumbest people in the Bible. In this particular story, two angels were commissioned by God to go on the worst babysitting mission ever, which was to save Lot's behind. This man was not an easy person to save. He is like the guy standing on the deck of a sinking ship playing shuffleboard, refusing to go into the lifeboat because of the color. Reading the above verses, you get a glimpse into Lot's situation. You undoubtedly know the story of Sodom and Gomorrah and their total destruction. Sodom is the city where Lot had chosen to live with his wife and two daughters. It was a lovely modern convenience community filled with a beautiful array of extreme sexual predators. The place was so utterly depraved that when God sent two angels to rescue the family, every single man, young and old, surrounded Lot's house with the intent of raping the angels. My first thought while reading this story was, *What?! Why are these people living here?*

The stupidity and cowardice continue when Lot, instead of being the hero of his family, decides the best thing to do is...throw his two virgin daughters out to the deranged mob. I want to punch him in the face. Apparently, God felt some of these same feelings. He stepped into the protective role for these women and struck all the men blind. This is the ship-sinking moment!

In Genesis 19:15-19, the angels tell Lot and his family to run. Lot lingers in the house–who knows why–but the angels literally must take him by the hand and lead him from the house. Once outside, the angels give Lot instructions to take his family to the mountain. "Escape for your life! Do not look behind you or stop anywhere in the entire valley; escape to the mountains [of Moab], or you will be consumed *and* swept away." I can almost hear Lot's nasally whine as he makes his objection. *Not the mountain! Please, allow me to go to Zoar. I am sure God just didn't see it, but it's a quaint picturesque village just below the mountain. Please, let me go where I want instead.*

God doesn't force Lot to listen to Him, he simply lets him go to Zoar. When they finally reach their precious village under the mountain, they hate it. Lot is so terrified of the people there; he ends up fleeing to the mountain. They ended up going to the very same place God originally chose for him! This is funny to me, that Lot actually believed he was more qualified than God to select his new home location. I mean, his last choice had been Sodom. Would you trust Lot to tell you where you should live? Absolutely not. He chose the worst place in all of human history, and He still felt that He was more qualified than God. Please, pause here to pass judgment over Lot. If you want extra credit, you can open your Bible and study him more–there are many more examples in his life of doing things the wrong way.

Now that we have looked at Lot, this is my moment to look in the mirror. How often have I whined, just like Lot, when God told me to *"Go to the mountain"*? I, in my infinite wisdom, often feel like I know so much better. Here is my Lot story.

My husband and I were leading a mission trip to Haiti and boarded the plane. The only other countries I had visited previously were Mexico and Canada. I was both nervous and excited to be going on this unknown adventure with God. I put my carry-on in the overhead compartment. Then sat next to the poor soul that would be sitting next to me for the flight. If you are not someone who likes to talk with random strangers on planes, then you may not understand. I am a writer and I absolutely love getting to hear people's stories. I always introduce myself and give this disclaimer, "Hello, my name is Jenny. Just wondering if you are interested in chatting or would you enjoy some quiet time by yourself?"

Almost everyone I have encountered while traveling is willing to engage in conversation, except for one time, when I was in the very last row on a plane and there was an elderly woman with knitting needles! I gave my spiel and waited to hear her response. She didn't say a word. She just glared at me and continued knitting. *Seriously, how did she get past security with those things?! They confiscated a small shampoo bottle from my purse, so how did this woman get past the metal detector with knitting needles? She probably stared the guard down, causing him to instantly collapse into the fetal position.*

Sorbe

You may not know this, but Johnson is quite sarcastic. Behind her sweet, flowery personality lies a hilariously sarcastic storyteller–completely g-rated, but funny, nonetheless. I will allow her to go on. Please continue Johnson, I am loving every minute of this!

Johnson

Thanks, Sorbe! Like I said, most people are willing to talk, and such was my good fortune on this particular trip. The gentleman seated next to me was an international soccer player from Germany. He was traveling to Haiti with other members of his team to teach kids soccer. The conversation was light and pleasant, until he realized I was a Christian. That is when the conversation took a surprise turn. He began to give a detailed list of everything he didn't like about Christians. Our discussion was mostly me listening and trying not to add to his reasons for hating Christians. Then I clearly heard God tell me to pray for this man. Instant panic! I pleaded with God, *Oh, no! Please God, no. Please do not ruin the rest of my flight! This man does not even like Christians; he doesn't want me to pray for him. He will get mad, and I will be forced to spend the rest of my flight in awkward silence.* God persisted, so I whined, *Please God, can I wait to pray for him? At least then I won't have to endure the awkwardness.* I know these were not God's exact words, but I can picture God rolling his eyes at me and sighing, *"Fine, Jenny, you can go to your village under the mountain."*

I immediately felt relief wash over my entire body. I relaxed into my seat and continued to listen. On a quick bonus note of stupid for your enjoyment...*why* was I excited to go on this trip in the first place? Answer: to step out in faith and follow God wherever he was leading, and I was anticipating Him moving in miraculous, awesome ways. This very moment was possibly the reason God had called me to go to Haiti in the first place, and I was missing it!

The plane was just about to begin its descent, and I knew I needed to do what I had promised. I nervously asked this famous soccer player if I could pray for him. He raised an annoyed eyebrow and huffed, "Sure." I could already feel the awkwardness descending upon me, but I did pray. I prayed blessings over his family, his career, his time in Haiti, and some other important things that I no longer remember, because it was all coming from the Holy Spirit. So, was I right? Did the painful awkward silence happen? Nope, the exact opposite. I looked up from my folded hands to find a complete shift in our conversation. He thanked me, over and over again for praying for him. He began asking me tons of excited questions about my faith in Christ. Our conversation was really just beginning and now it was time to exit the plane. As we grabbed our luggage from the overhead bins, his questions continued. We talked until we were forced to join our individual groups to process through customs; just a few precious minutes, and he was gone, and our conversation was over.

WHEN GOD ORDERS YOU TO REMOVE SOMETHING FROM YOUR LIFE, CHUCK IT!

As I look back and reflect on that event, I am forced to ask myself some important questions. What if I had prayed when God asked me to? Why did I think, much like Lot, that I knew better? Honestly, I am hearing the voice of my mother-in-law right now. "Delayed obedience is disobedience." When my children wouldn't respond to my instructions immediately, my mother-in-law would jump in with these words. I can hear her voice sometimes and in moments like this realize the profound wisdom in taking them to heart. That is the lesson to be learned from these two stories. When God says run from Sodom and Gomorrah, RUN...do not linger. When God says pack your things and go to the mountain, go to the mountain. When God says pray for the stranger next to you on the plane, pray. When God orders you to remove something from your life, chuck it! I can promise you that not obeying always has negative consequences. You want a life free of regret? Listen and obey. God's way will always be better than yours...always.

Sorbe

We read that the angels woke Lot up and urged them all to get moving. I believe that the Lord was urging me through my dream, to reach out to the Johnson family. But like Lot, I shrugged it off. Even though it pressed into my mind and was unique enough to compel me to share it with my husband, I chose to put it on a shelf to deal with later (or if I'm being honest, ignore). It felt silly to think a dream could matter. But God knew me and thankfully reached out again. In my hesitation to obey, God was merciful, just as He was merciful to Lot's family with their delayed obedience.

TRUTH IS, YOU MISS OUT ON 100% OF THE BLESSINGS IF YOU NEVER TRY.

There have been several times when I have felt the urging of the Holy Spirit to say or do something, but I chose not to engage. Most often the reason? Fear. *What if what I am hearing or feeling is not from God after all and I make a fool of myself?* I have downplayed my relationship with Jesus in the past, afraid of rejection. However, if I never step out of my comfort zone in these areas, I will never learn to discern what is, in fact, God's nudging. What if God will use your obedience to open a new opportunity? Truth is, you miss out on 100% of the blessings if you never try. Like Johnson shared in her airplane story above, she vacillated on whether she should obey God's urgings. She feared awkward silence. Funny how our mind seems to want to go to the negative consequences rather than the hope of a positive outcome! Jenny learned from her experience that obedience is rewarded with an opportunity to pray and share the gospel. Her delay stole some of her time experiencing that unique blessing of being used by God in another person's life. In contrast when we obey this call, God receives the glory, and we receive the blessing. Thankfully, God is merciful and patient with us. Have patience and receive God's gracious forgiveness when you miss or ignore those moments, but don't let it stop you from stepping back in or praying about that missed opportunity. Instead of allowing immobilizing guilt to *shame* you (*not from God*), ask Him to give you another opportunity. Then step out in faith believing God has a good plan. Pray for courage! Ask to hear and know God's voice. And guess what will happen?

THE MORE YOU STEP OUT OF
YOUR COMFORT ZONE, THE MORE
COMFORTABLE YOU WILL BECOME
BEING UNCOMFORTABLE.

The more you step out of your comfort zone, the more comfortable you will become being uncomfortable.

"Awkward is awesome."
Jen Johnson

Group Discussion Questions/Action Step/ Personal Reflection/Journal:

- Consider the term "stupid." Does this word have a positive or negative connotation for you?

- Do you have a "stupid," not listening to God, moment to share? There's no guilt or shame here! The purpose of this question is to reflect on where you are with God right now. What can you learn from your story?

- Sorbe talked about fear keeping us from doing what God tells us...what keeps you from fully trusting God?

Assignment: Write a bold prayer to confront your hesitation.

Prayer:

Dear Jesus,

I am realizing You are much smarter than me and that Your ways are better than my ways. Forgive me for doing it my way. Holy Spirit, reveal to me how to be bold in my faith and obey You in the moment without hesitation. I want to walk out my faith in new and exciting ways. Thank you for Your forgiveness!

In Jesus' name I pray. Amen

OPEN

"Most of us ask God for a life free of pain, a life of comfort. No one who was living for God in the Bible was called to a comfortable life. No adventure story revolves around the pursuit of complacent living."
Johnson

"When they cry for help, I will not answer. Though they anxiously search for me (Wisdom), they will not find me. For they hated knowledge and chose not to fear the Lord. They rejected my advice and paid no attention when I corrected them. Therefore, they must eat the bitter fruit of living their own way, choking on their own schemes. For simpletons turn away from me-to death. Fools are destroyed by their own complacency. But all who listen to me (Wisdom) will live in peace, untroubled by fear of harm."
Proverbs 1:28-33 (NLT)

Open:[1]

1 : having no enclosing or confining barrier; accessible on all or nearly all sides
2 : being in a position or adjustment to permit passage; not shut or locked

3–START WITH OPEN

"We are agents of omnipotence. This means that unlimited power is at our fingertips...there is a great God at work in human beings who have childlike faith."
Reinhard Bonnke, (Even Greater)

"I write these things to you who believe in the name of the Son of God, that you may know that you have eternal life. And this is the confidence that we have toward him, that if we ask anything according to his will he hears us. And if we know that he hears us in whatever we ask, we know that we have the requests that we have asked of him."
1 John 5:13-15 (ESV)

Johnson

Open. Vulnerability. Obedience. In these next three chapters, we will dive into these concepts. Let's start with vulnerability...

The very first retreat Sorbe and I were invited to speak at was "Women, Horses, and Healing[1]." It is a ministry where ladies who have experienced sexual abuse, emotional/physical trauma connect with Jesus in a powerful healing environment. As I prepared for this event, I knew God was asking me to share a very personal traumatic memory and, though I was learning to trust the voice of the Holy Spirit, I did not want to obey Him. I was mentally wrestling with God over what He wanted me to do. I heard Him say, "Jenny, I want you to be vulnerable. I want you to read the section in your high school diary that you are the most afraid of sharing. Make no excuses or explanations. "In the past I struggled to not be overly apologetic. I was afraid of people's perception of me. I never wanted to cause drama or offend. I was constantly apologizing for speaking my thoughts. The Holy Spirit was inviting me into a level of obedience and trust that made me very uncomfortable. He was telling me to share truthfully and release myself from the worries that normally plagued me. When I walked in the door of the retreat's beautiful lake cabin, immediately, I was greeted by a petite athletic blond. She boldly took my hand and shook it, "Hi, I'm Abbey. I was a drug addict, and Jesus totally saved my life! And...vulnerability is awesome!"

———†———

JESUS SHOT RIGHT PAST MY DEFENSES
AND WENT STRAIGHT FOR MY HEART!

—————————

Jesus shot right past my defenses and went straight for my heart! Abbey's words hit me, obliterating all my excuses. She was not ashamed of God and the powerful way in which He saved her! This petite woman was a shining light for Christ, imparting the courage I needed to push beyond my fear. I read my diary and made no excuses or explanations. It was powerful and healing.

That night God used my reluctant vulnerability and obedience to draw me closer to Him. The ladies shared their own personal stories, we cried, hugged, and prayed over one another. It was powerful! Jesus and Abbey taught me that vulnerability and openness with God is actually awesome!

Sorbe

I want to start by saying; I absolutely love Abbey and her bold courageous faith! Vulnerability is strength, not a weakness. I began learning this through my interactions with Jenny. Because of her great suffering, I felt vulnerable and unqualified to help her. I knew God was asking me to step into prayer in a greater way than I had ever done. I needed to learn...and learn quickly! I knew I had to start somewhere; but, I felt like I didn't have the time. Evenings were hard because they always seemed to be stolen by the needs of my kids or my own household duties and distractions. I longed to get up before my family and invest time into learning and listening to God but there was a pattern of thinking that was preventing me from following through. I was a self-proclaimed night owl and did not *want* to change my behavior.

IT WAS TIME FOR ME TO ADJUST MY THINKING PATTERN AND BE OPEN TO CHANGE.

Morning people made such a big deal about how much more they got accomplished. For years I had decided they were wrong. There I was, not adapting, and failing to make the time I truly needed to get into the presence of God without interruption. So, what did I do? I watched a YouTube video on how to wake up early. Ha! The common theme was to set your alarm for 6:00 A.M. and not hit snooze. It would hurt the first couple of days until the rhythm set in; but, with a little consistency, it would feel great, and you'd accomplish so much more. It was time for me to adjust my thinking pattern and be *open* to change.

Often, we want to better our lives, but we won't make the necessary changes to actually accomplish it. We *must* be open to new ideas. Sometimes those ideas are initially challenging to step into, but in the end pay great dividends. So...open I became. And you know what? Waking up early really did help me accomplish more in my day. It immediately set the tone and put me on a firm foundation. Though I was waking up much earlier, I was less tired throughout the day. I began devouring books on prayer. Sometimes, I just sat there quietly sipping my coffee; thinking or listening to whatever God might say to me. My life was getting better. I was learning so much! I was beginning to sense God's leading; it was getting exciting! Morning people were right after all! I take back all the awful things I thought or said about them.

Alright, let's define the word open, shall we? When you open a can of soup, you peel the whole lid back to get to the contents inside. What about when you open a door to a room? How about opening your hand to receive the hand of someone else? The more open these things are, the easier it is to get to the contents inside, to walk through or to receive. Open your hand for me right now. Do it fully, then partially, and observe how it looks both ways. There's something vulnerable in opening it all the way. Do you feel that? Do it again. Can you feel the difference? Fully opening your hand to receive another's, be it man or God, is like a portrayal of complete surrender or submission to trust. This is the picture I began to see in my mind as God was leading me to be fully open to Him. The interesting thing is I thought I had been open to Him until I felt compelled to actually pray and say, "Lord, have your way with me and my life, with my family and my home. I am fully open to you and I trust you." Gulp. That, I am embarrassed to say, was NOT easy for me to pray. I started to realize that I was partially open to God, but not fully. I was terrified to pray that prayer. Numerous thoughts would spin through my head, such as, "as soon as you say you're open, Jenn, God will take one of your children from you so you can learn how to love Him more. He will have you suffer to teach you lessons. If you're completely open, you'll have to become poor. You'll need to move to a third world country and be a missionary."

On and on down the slippery slope my thoughts and fears took me. In order for me to open up my hands completely to God, I needed to trust His character. But what is that? I would have to dive into scripture to find out. Without knowing God's true character and really knowing He is good, no one in their right mind would open themselves up to that stuff needlessly. You see, God is good, but often I would hear these types of things in my thoughts, "But is He really?" How about I give Him most of me and the rest I'll just hold onto; because, after all, I love my children best and I trust me the most.

In Dutch Sheets' book, *Watchman Prayer*, he states, "So many people do not understand God's heart toward His kids. He is waiting, longing for a visit; they are waiting to be 'shot.'

Controlled by our own fears and distorted perceptions of who God really is, we rob ourselves and Him of the pleasure He intended for the relationship."[2] It is hard to admit to ourselves or others when we don't trust Him fully, but for how many of us is this true?" It sure was true for me.

The prophet Jeremiah tells us we will "seek Him and find Him" when we "search for Him with all our heart."[3] Jeremiah precedes this with a powerful declaration from the Lord concerning His view *towards us* and His plans *for us*: "For I know the plans I have for you," declares the Lord, "plans to prosper you and not to harm you, plans to give you hope and a future."[4] He wants PROSPERITY for us! Yes, you heard that right–prosperity. The Hebrew word for prosperity is shalom. Most of you know that shalom typically means "peace," but it is also defined as "perfect, whole, complete, prosperous, harmonious and tranquil." Are you lacking in peace? Hope? Trust? Patience? Prosperity? God wants to give you what you lack. Imagine your thought life entirely free of fear, worry, poverty, and doubt... This is what God plans for us. It's not prosperity in things, though sometimes fleshly rewards come with it, it is prosperity IN HIM! Take a moment to go back up and read what God desires for you. Read it out loud and KNOW its God's heart FOR YOU.

I will tell you this: the thoughts I had racing through my mind were *not* thoughts based on the true character of God; but a skewed view of Him... and the circular argument in my head was being filtered through fear.

Johnson

"Hard to admit that we don't trust Him fully, but for how many of us is this true?" Sorbe posed such a great question when she talked about her struggle with being fully open to God. Her roadblock to being open was rooted in fear, whereas my

struggle with being open brought another word to mind...*control*. Sorbe and I are different in several ways. Because of her military background, she isn't afraid to swear to prove her point. I, on the other hand, do not swear. Sorbe may partake in the occasional glass of wine. I do not drink. I do not even remotely like the taste or smell of alcohol. Sorbe will drink her steaming cup of highly caffeinated coffee to give her a burst of energy in the morning. I try my utmost to escape dependence on caffeine. Sorbe is a very disciplined soldier and thoughtful planner. I feel confined by planning. I jump into situations and figure things out as I go. All these idiosyncrasies of mine are not necessarily bad, but they do point to a glaring weakness: I love to be in control.

Swearing, to me, represents a loss of control over my emotions. Wine might change my mood or make me feel relaxed. Caffeine might create dependence. Control...even the word brings comfort. It is like sitting by a campfire, wrapped within a plaid blanket, cradling a warm cup of hot cocoa with tiny marshmallows floating in it. We see independent, self-control mantras plastered everywhere. "You can do anything if you put your mind to it" "Weak women ask for help." "Be strong and self-sufficient." With fists raised, I scream, "I want to be a strong, independent woman!"

Sorbe

Pardon me for a moment. I just giggle here as I imagine Johnson raising her fists and screaming, "I am a strong, independent woman!" I have affectionately described Johnson as butterflies and balloons. Even when she is angry, people still want to hug her. But let me tell you, Johnson is a pretty tough cookie!

Johnson

Sorbe does call me "butterflies and balloons," and I laugh every time. Just so you know, I call her Rambo Barbie!

My pride and doing things *my way* is my own special kind of stupid. This strong will and desire to be "independent" has been a barrier between God and me. I have two stories to share with you concerning how this attitude keeps us from letting God and others into our hearts, minds, and souls.

In kindergarten, my dear father held out his hand in a protective gesture to walk me across the street to school. I pulled my hand away and declared, "I can hold my own hand!" I distinctly remember the fear that if my friends observed me walking to school while holding my father's hand, I would be judged. After all, I was a big kid...needing help was for babies. At 5 years old, I had decided that instead of finding security in my father's love, I would prove to him (and my friends) I was big enough to lead and protect myself. God is a good father, reaching out His hand daily to us. He desires to walk personally with us, our hand in His. There is precious security and love found in holding the hand of our Heavenly Father. This is the picture of giving Him control.

"Without knowing God's true character and truly knowing He is good, no one in their right mind would open themselves up." Sorbe's words from above are an excellent intro to my next story. Let me take a moment to clarify something... putting our faith into untrustworthy people is not what God is asking of us. God is like a forest ranger, guiding lost hikers to food and shelter. We read in Proverbs 16:9 that in our heart we plan our own way, but *the Lord is the one* who establishes our steps. He is the One qualified to lead us and we can trust Him to do it purposefully, with love. Psalm 23:4 says, "Yea, though I walk through the valley of the shadow of death, I will fear no evil; For You *are* with me; Your rod and Your staff, they comfort me (NKJV)." Not only is God going to

lead you, but He is going to comfort you and give you the tools needed to walk through the valleys.

This story came about during my high school years, when my parents took me camping in the Boundary Waters. Now, if you don't know...the Boundary Waters is hardcore camping. It offers a true wilderness experience. It is not the "bring your camper to a campsite filled with many comforts" kind of camping. People have died in these woods. Okay, so there is the overly dramatic build-up for this story. Anyway, we pushed off from shore, leaving early in the morning with mist rising up all around our canoes. We paddled across cloudy green water for maybe an hour and parked our boats in front of a dirt path. My dad laid out instructions for how we were going to get to our campsite. He explained that everyone needed to carry something, because we had to portage our gear and supplies to another lake. My hand shot into the air, and I boldly declared that I would carry the canoe. My dad raised an eyebrow and turned his full attention to me. "Jenny, are you sure you want to do that? I can carry the canoe. It is heavy and we have a long day ahead."

I imagine that I puffed myself up in all my scrawny, red-headed, freckle-faced glory and spoke in a confident, adolescent tone, "I can do it! It's easy." My dad shook his head and allowed me to carry the canoe. It was awful. In my infinite wisdom, I had worn shorts. This is a problem considering I knew full well the Boundary Waters are blessed with a constant, replenishing supply of mosquitoes. The path I walked was hilly and uneven; it was littered with roots and rocks. I became the mosquitoes' smorgasbord whilst carrying the canoe. I could not slap those vampire insects away as they injected themselves deep into my skin, turning my legs a nice shade of gray. The sound of the mosquito is a thousand times more annoying than that of a fly because it comes with a promise of relentless itching. My dad followed behind me. No matter how hard things got, I marched on without complaint. There was no way I was going to give in and ask him for help! Upon reaching the shoreline, I dropped the canoe and began smacking myself in frantic pinwheel motions.

My dad assessed my situation with a concerned frown and asked, "Are you alright?" My response should have been, "Dad, I need aloe! I need calamine lotion! I should have worn pants like you suggested before we left home!" Instead, I replied, "I am doing great! I'm ready to head to the campsite." Dumb, dumb, dumb. Because of this decision, I spent the first couple of nights tossing and turning in a state of constant misery, consumed by my self-inflicted wounds. In my heart, it was worth it. Though I was sure my display of strength had impressed my dad, the reality was that my father could see my struggle and was by no means impressed by my rebellious, prideful stupidity. He merely wanted to bond with his daughter on a family camping trip. I had missed the point: the journey was meant to be walked together.

Sorbe

You know Johnson, we're never really fooling anyone when we try to fake it; especially those who know us best. *"The journey was meant to be walked together."* Yes! The journey absolutely IS meant to be walked together. Relationships are the point. Good ones require vulnerability. Admitting when we need help, instead of pretending we have it all together, is honest and healing. Good, Godly friendships sharpen us. I would like to take a moment to walk you down memory lane to a younger me and admit my own stupid thinking.

I was the first born of two. My mother said I was a strong-willed child. In other words, I put my will before others, and it was hard for my parents to guide me. I was stubborn. Because of this, I spent plenty of time in a timeout chair. Anyone else experienced this, too? (I've heard it said that strong-willed kids make great leaders one day, but they're a challenge to rear up in the way they should go. My poor parents. God bless them.) I had an admirable mom who held me accountable for my lousy actions, bad attitude, and back-talking mouth. Once on my chair, I could be released if I apologized for my wrongdoing. However, I didn't much like to apologize. Admitting my wrong felt awful, so blaming the other person was my way to deflect the icky feeling. Pride (stubbornness) would rise up to cover the vulnerable feeling of guilt or shame. *'You can discipline me, and I will take it without a fuss, but you won't win my mind. I will not be sorry.'* This is how I thought I took control. I willed myself to believe I was right and everyone else was wrong.

Since I wouldn't apologize, and thus earn my freedom, I had a lot of time to think about things. One time I did something bad enough to get a spanking from my dad. He rarely spanked me, so this really offended me and struck my pride. He sent me to another room to cool off. In all my hot anger, I pondered how I could get back at him for the perceived offense. I noticed the electrical socket on the wall and knew I wasn't supposed to put my fingers in it or I would get electrocuted. I was emotional, indignant, selfish, and bent on retaliation. I stuck my two little kid fingers in the socket. A jolt of electricity coursed through my arm and down my spine and my little body was knocked backwards. It hurt and it scared me. I was immediately embarrassed. It was silly to think that by hurting myself I could somehow hurt my dad. I'm laughing right now as I write this. It seems ridiculous to me now of course. Obviously if the outcome had been worse, they certainly would have been hurt by my actions. My goal was not to hurt myself at all, rather it was to hurt them. What was I trying to prove by my actions? My pride was at stake, and I didn't want to deal with what I had done. I didn't want to learn from my mistakes because it's painful to admit things that make you look bad to another person. It felt way easier to just be angry and lash out. It felt courageous and redemptive to hurt myself in order to hurt them. Sadly, it only proved to harm, embarrass, and shame me all the more. I can guarantee you my father would not have wanted me to be in shame. He would have wanted me to learn a lesson to save my future self. Unfortunately, I did not *want* to own up to my wrongdoing. I was unteachable and immovable in my thinking. Rather than listening to and learning from a father who held me accountable for my actions and loved me enough to discipline me, I allowed my pride to rule. In the end, I chose a stupid solution that ultimately brought *me* pain.

Looking back on that day, I can see how I let offense come into play and gave it ownership to rule over my emotions; no amount of truth would have mattered to me. It reminds me of the verses in Romans 8:6-11 where Paul is talking about how, when we allow our sinful nature to control our minds, it leads to death. Jeremiah 29:11 shows us the beautiful characteristics of God our Father. I had a wonderful earthly father, some of you may not have. God is not our earthly father. He is our heavenly father. He wants to give us life and to give us life abundantly (John 10:10). Thank you, Jesus.

Through my adolescent years my mother taught me about Jesus and how to have a personal relationship with Him. In the mornings before school, as I was eating or doing my hair, she would read the Bible to me–pouring God's Word into my very soul. What I was hearing was in opposition to everything my sinful desire wanted to be: strong-willed, prideful, dominant, and rebellious. I didn't want to listen, yet I couldn't help but listen. I didn't want to be told to turn the other cheek. I didn't want to give somebody a cloak after they'd just stolen from me. No, I did not want to be humble. That felt weak and powerless. Submit to authority? But what if I thought their rules didn't apply to me? The thing was, God knew me and wanted me. He drew me to Him at a very young age. I still remember the moment I asked Jesus to come into my life and take me into His family. Alone, in the kitchen, I walked over to the window seat. I mimicked the old man in the photo I'd seen praying over his loaf of bread. As I kneeled and pressed my palms together, I peered up into the sky and said, *"Jesus, I love you. I would like for you to please come into my heart forever."* I may have said a few other things, but I remember smiling and knowing that I had done something special, and I was going to heaven. Off I jumped onto the floor and up to my room to play. Now in my adolescence, as I am hearing my mom read to me, His words were putting cracks into my strong will. My unteachable and immovable thinking was being assailed. The wall around my stubborn and prideful heart was beginning to crumble. I fell head over heels in love with Him and all I can say now is, thank God I did. Had He not given me the mother I had, and a father who was willing to spank my butt when I needed it, I do not know what kind of mess I would be in today.

The battle for my mind would be great. Jesus had won my heart, but the enemy of Jesus would lie to me and too many times I would believe the lies. However, throughout my years, God's Word would speak His loving truth into my very soul, working hard to replace those lies. The fight to be *open* was on.

Johnson

———†———

WHOSE HAND ARE YOU GOING TO LET LEAD YOU - JESUS OR SATAN'S? IT'S ONE OR THE OTHER. THERE IS NO MIDDLE GROUND.

Sorbe's mother, lovingly reading scripture over her, was in stark opposition to her doing things her own way. Following Jesus often begins with a battle of wills. Whose hand are you going to let lead you–Jesus or satan's? It's one or the other. There is no middle ground. James 4:4 says friendship with the world is choosing to be an enemy to God. If we're not living God's way, then we are living satan's way.

Simply being in the Lord's presence changes us, just like Sorbe's mom reading scripture changed her. Moses also walked with God, and it made his face shine. Moses had some stupid moments, but he is a great example of being open. Let's read Exodus 4:10-14 (NLT).

> *"But Moses pleaded with the Lord, 'O Lord, I'm not very good with words. I never have been, and I'm not now, even though you have spoken to me. I get tongue-tied, and my words get tangled.' "Then the Lord asked Moses, 'Who makes a person's mouth? Who decides whether people speak or do not speak, hear or do not hear, see or do not see? Is it not I, the Lord? Now go! I will be with you as you speak, and I will instruct you in what to say.' "But Moses again pleaded, "Lord, please! Send anyone else." Then the Lord became angry with Moses. "All right," he said. "What about your brother, Aaron the Levite? I know he speaks well. And look! He is on his way to meet you now. He will be delighted to see you"*

A quick summary of what is happening here... Moses is an eighty-year-old man and God is telling him to step into his calling as a mouthpiece. The day has finally arrived for the Lord to free His people from slavery in Egypt! What an exciting historical moment! How does Moses react? He doesn't want to do it. Moses pleads, begging God to send someone else. He is not open to doing what the Creator of the universe is asking of him, because he is too focused on his own lack of abilities. God, all through chapter 4, explains how He will speak *for* Moses. Not only will God ultimately be the one talking, but He even gives Moses the ability to do miraculous signs to show people if they don't believe him. All these assurances were not enough to convince this to-be-prophet to obey. It was not until God allowed Aaron to go with him to speak, did Moses finally become open to doing what God had asked. This is utter foolishness! Imagine Moses saying this to God: "God, your promise of going with me isn't enough. I need something more than you. I think your plan is stupid because it includes me, could you just send someone who is better qualified in public speaking?"

Moses was literally raised in a palace, given the finest education only a royal birth could provide; and, in effect he was being trained for this assignment his whole life. However, he would rather ditch God's plans and simply be a sheep herder?! Whose plan is better? Moses should have understood that, in comparison to God, Aaron was a poor substitution to the Lord. Thankfully the Bible is full of redeeming moments, and Moses experienced a significant one in Exodus 33:12-18 (NKJV),

> *"Then Moses said to the Lord, 'See, You say to me, 'Bring up this people.' But You have not let me know whom You will send with me. Yet You have said, 'I know you by name, and you have also found grace in My sight.' Now therefore, I pray, if I have found grace in Your sight, show me now Your way, that I may know You and that I may find grace in Your sight. And consider that this nation is Your people. "And He said, "My Presence will go with you, and I will give you rest. "Then he said to Him, 'If Your Presence does not go with us, do not bring us up from here. For how then will it be known that Your people and I have found grace in Your sight, except You go with us? So we shall be separate, Your people and I, from all the people who are upon the*

face of the earth.' "So the Lord said to Moses, 'I will also do this thing that you have spoken; for you have found grace in My sight, and I know you by name.' "And he said, 'Please, show me Your glory'".

WOW! What a change of heart! Moses went from God's presence feeling not good enough, to begging God for more of His presence. What changed? Moses had gained a real relationship with God. The words used in Exodus 33:11 say the Lord spoke to Moses as one would a friend. This once reluctant prophet or "man baby" was transformed into a respected man of God who became a true patriarch of Israel. Moses witnessed and participated in God's miraculous deliverance of his people out of slavery. He walked on dry land when God parted the waters of the Red Sea, followed by the drowning of Pharaoh's army in those very same waters. He spent over 40 days on Mount Sinai, spending time alone with God listening and memorizing His law.

Sorbe

I like that; *spending time alone with God, listening and memorizing His Word.* How much will we mature and see our fears and insecurities fall off when we do the same, I wonder...

Johnson

Moses did not begin his assignment being fully open to God, but it was the beginning of what would become a much deeper friendship. You may be in a Moses space right now, nervous about what God has planned for you. That is okay. Moses did not fully trust God, and even in his reluctant obedience God still used him and changed his heart along the way.

Moses was physically affected by His encounter with God. His face shone so brightly people were afraid to look at him. Even at his death at 120 years old, he had clear vision and his natural vigor never left him.[4] Can you imagine any person living to be 120 being described in such a way? Walking with, listening to, and obeying God will transform you in all the best ways. If you are ready, please say these words from Exodus 33 with me; *"Now therefore, I pray, if I have found grace in Your sight, show me now Your way... Please God, show me Your Glory."*

"Lord, have your way in me," has been a prayer echoed by many believers throughout history. It is a great example for us as we begin to be more open to God in everything. 2 Corinthians 3:4-18 paints a beautiful picture of this before we move on to the next two chapters. Please feel free to read the whole thing in your Bible or enjoy this little piece...

> *"But whenever someone turns to the Lord, the veil is taken away. For the Lord is the Spirit, and wherever the Spirit of the Lord is, there is* ***freedom****. So all of us who have had that veil removed can see and reflect the glory of the Lord. And the Lord—who is the Spirit—makes us more and more like him as we are changed into his glorious image."*
>
> 2 Corinthians 3:16-18 (NLT)

Being OPEN to God will absolutely transform you. You may even start to glow! Being a literal light for Jesus sounds pretty awesome.

Group Discussion Questions/Action Step/ Personal Reflection/Journal:

Open:[6]

1 : having no enclosing or confining barrier: accessible on all or nearly all sides.
2 : being in a position or adjustment to permit passage: not shut or locked.

Our prayer for you, as we enter into the questions, is that your life will reflect the above definition. We pray all barriers between you and God will be removed, because they are keeping you from being completely open to Him. Let's practice being open together!

- Examine the definition above. What may be preventing you from being open with God right now? Is there fear or a feeling of not being qualified? Let's ask the Holy Spirit right now to reveal what thoughts may be holding you back. (The Holy Spirit will often talk to you with a picture, a thought, or a memory.)

- Speak out loud this prayer right now:

"Holy Spirit, I invite you to speak to me. Reveal to me anything in my life that may be hindering You from fully working in and through me." (Listen quietly. What do you feel, hear, or see in your mind?)

If you don't hear or see anything, don't be discouraged. There is power in our words. Try asking the Holy Spirit out loud[7], "Holy Spirit, why don't I see or hear anything?" or "Holy Spirit, what is blocking me from hearing you right now?" (Listen quietly. What do you hear or see in your mind?)

Most of us do not hear an audible voice speaking to us, but we can hear or sense a thought or word(s) that connect us with what we are seeking answers for. Whatever we feel or hear we can bring to the Lord in prayer. Prayer brings revelation, understanding, and freedom.

Assignment: All through God's Word we are told how important prayer is. Matthew 18:19-20 says that if two of us agree here on earth concerning what we ask the Lord for, our Father in heaven will do it. He even goes as far as saying that He is among those who pray together. Prayer is powerful, but prayer with other believers is even better. We encourage you to do the next step with a friend if you can.

- Open your hands and tell God you are open to Him, ready to receive whatever He has for you. If you have any doubts about God's good character, go ahead and ask Him to reveal His true character to you. Ask to have eyes to see and ears to hear what He wants to reveal to you. Be open.

- Write down anything God taught you, said to you, or did during the day.

Prayer:

Dear Jesus,

I purpose and choose to be open to You. I confess all fear that I've had fully opening up to You. I ask You to forgive me for not trusting You to take care of me. I receive Your forgiveness now and I cancel all lies that I have believed that have kept me from being fully open with You. Lord, please show me Your true character and remove any faulty thinking I have about you. Give me eyes to see and ears to hear what you are revealing to me. Lord protect me, guide me, and speak to me. I am open.

In Jesus' Name, Amen

4–BE OPEN

"My passion is to be consumed with him and not cling to my own "righteousness" based in keeping the written Law. My only "righteousness" will be his, based on the faithfulness of Jesus Christ—the very righteousness that comes from God. And I continually long to know the wonders of Jesus and to experience the overflowing power of his resurrection working in me. I will be one with him in his sufferings and become like him in his death. Only then will I be able to experience complete oneness with him in his resurrection from the realm of death."
Philippians 3:9-11 (TPT)

"[To have Faith in Christ] means, of course, trying to do all that He says. There would be no sense in saying you trusted a person if you would not take his advice. Thus if you have really handed yourself over to Him, it must follow that you are trying to obey Him. But trying in a new way, a less worried way. Not doing these things in order to be saved, but because He has begun to save you already. Not hoping to get to Heaven as a reward for your actions, but inevitably wanting to act in a certain way because a first faint gleam of Heaven is already inside you."
C.S. Lewis, (Mere Christianity)

Sorbe

What stupid stories are you reminded of in your own life as you read these priceless moments from our lives? I'm so thankful that my Lord is a patient God who wants what is best for me (2 Peter 3:8-9, Isaiah 30:18). Why is saving face so important to us? Why is vulnerability so scary? Ask yourself right now what you are hiding from others. Did you recently tell a half-truth to cover up something you were afraid to let someone know? I've done it, you've done it; honestly, it is common practice. Isn't it funny how we are offended when someone lies to us, but are we guilty of the same? The irony is not lost on me. So, where do we draw the line in the sand? I'm asking you a lot of questions here, I know. Flow with me, will you for a moment? What if we were always completely honest? What would that look like in a relationship? I can tell you I have very rarely ever known a relationship that honest. I mean, we may be mostly honest...but COMPLETELY honest? Can you be completely honest and say whether you have ever been consistently, day in and day out, completely transparent? Not me! But I want to be. Why? Because that is real. That is true.

My friends and I call this concept "sharing our last 5 %." You know, the 5% of our thoughts no one knows because it's that secret ugly part that makes us look bad. Let me give you an example from my own life. Johnson and I are friends. We do ministry together. We pray together. We talk often. But for a while, I was not being fully honest with her. I wasn't exactly lying, but I wasn't being upfront either. Jenny had organized our very first speaking engagement. She was over the moon excited about it. I, on the other hand, was not happy about it. I was fearful that I had nothing of value to share with these ladies and didn't want to let them down. I feared they would be all excited to hear from me, only to leave the event disappointed after realizing I really am not that great. My self-preservation pride was on high alert; and, though I had ample opportunity to let her know how I was truly feeling, I allowed her to believe I was going to the event by not saying anything. In reality, I was planning on 'leaving her at the altar' so-to-speak. A week before the event, I was going to give her a last-minute excuse as to why I couldn't go and wish her well with my best godly prayer. It was all planned out. *This is how a lie goes; it starts small and then it grows, and we must feed it to keep it alive. Sad.*

God was not about to let me miss out on this opportunity to grow in faith. He began working on my heart by causing me to feel the burden of my (deception) lie. I tried to rationalize that I was loving her by allowing her to be excited about the event and not sharing my negative attitude. However, the Holy Spirit was revealing to me how I was trying to prevent Johnson from seeing who I really was inside. A scared, self-centered coward. Please tell me this is not just a *me* thing...have you put yourself in this same uncomfortable position?

NO FLOWERS, NO RATIONALIZATIONS, JUST THE TRUTH. NO ANGER OR BLAME. NOPE, NONE OF THAT GARBAGE!

As I mentioned, God began to impress upon my spirit that I had to be completely truthful about where my mind was concerning this event. I would not make something up this time. I had to admit to her that I didn't want to go, admit that I ultimately didn't trust God to speak through me and use me, and that I had obvious self-esteem problems. Complete and unadulterated honesty. The five percent. The very essence of vulnerability. No flowers, no rationalizations, just the truth. No anger or blame. Nope, none of that garbage! This was a me-issue, as hard as that was to admit to myself, it was going to be even more difficult to admit to someone else. Every one of these, *blame and deflect and I won't look as bad,* garbage thoughts passed through my self-preserving, fear-soaked brain.

GOD WAS MOVING AND THE DEVIL HATED IT.

As the Lord was working on my heart, I began to realize I was partnering with fear and unbelief. Fear that I had nothing of value to offer these women and unbelief that I can do all things through Christ who gives me strength (Philippians 4:13). The devil wanted me to believe I would fail. He wanted to break up this powerful, Spirit-filled friendship. I mean, we were praying about things nearly every day! God was moving and the devil hated it. I was blind to it until I allowed the Holy Spirit to speak truth into my growing bitterness.

Seriously guys, I'm not over-dramatizing. This is how fear works. We get selfish. We start to blame. We want to save face. It's awful. I'm guessing you've either done what I'm talking about, or you've had it done to you.

The truth about truth is that it is actually a form of love. It forces us to self-reflect and own up to our ugliness, admitting it fully. The pain of our admission usually provides us with the best life lesson we will ever learn. God tells us in John 8:31-32, if we abide in His Word, we will know the truth and that truth will set us free. FREE! Not in bondage to fear, but FREE from it! The devil SOOO does not want us to get this understanding. He will lose every battle if we get this. Keep those secrets in the dark so no one will see the real ugly you, and the devil can keep you in bondage forever. Nope. You are learning that the truth will set you free and not one of us truly wants to be chained up. I heard the evangelist Mario Murillo once say, "God says the truth will set you free. He never said it would feel good or be easy...He said it would set you free." Hear, hear!

I knew sharing what my mind had been thinking in all its vulnerability and ugliness was going to make me look really bad. I even wondered if Johnson would want to be in partnership with me still. I knew if I was going to do this ministry–not for me, but for the Lord–and if I was going to be a true friend to Johnson, then I needed her to see me–ugly and all. No more lies, no more cover ups. The truth follows you whether you speak it out loud or not. It is always sitting right there as your constant companion to either shame you (the devil's way) or free you (God's way). In fact, I started noticing a pattern in my behavior, and it was not pretty.

SOMETIMES WE, TOO, PREFER THE DARKNESS OF DENIAL TO THE LIGHT OF TRUTH.

"Sometimes we, too, prefer the darkness of denial to the light of truth. Though the truth really does hurt at times, it is still truth. Denial does not change it. Where satan has made gains, let's admit it and determine to take them back!"[1] Yes, my thoughts exactly, Dutch. In John 8, Jesus is sharing with the people, including the Pharisees and the adulterous woman, that He is the Light of the World. They would find out that if they would choose Christ, they too would be the very vessels that bring His light to the world.

"I am the light of the world. Whoever follows me will not walk in darkness but will have the light of life" John 8:12 (ESV). Wow. We will have the *light of life* in us! But...not if I am going to have that darkness keep leading my mind and allowing lies and fear to rule me. God was showing me some truth and, though that truth was ugly, He wanted to set me FREE! I knew this. But I was scared.

We were a month out from the event, my name and face were on their website, and it was sold out. Every day I heard God gently urging me to be honest. Every day, I put it off for another day. Until one Sunday morning when I deliberately asked the Holy Spirit to give me something from the sermon that I could use to help me be completely honest with Johnson. I would obey and call her to tell her I wasn't going. God hears our prayers (1 John 5:15).

I took a deep breath and went to church. Boy, do I wish I could put a photo here of the slides up on the screen that morning, but one of them literally said, "Do not lie to your friends." *WHAT?* I laughed in my seat and thanked God for answering my prayer that morning. Later that day, I fulfilled my commitment to God. I called my friend and ministry partner and told her the truth. "I'm not going to the women's retreat." I honestly informed her, "I was planning to make an excuse at the last minute to get out of it. I'm so very sorry. You are going to have to do this one alone. I'm not ready and If I'm going to be completely truthful, I don't even want to go." I chuckled self-consciously and mentioned my prayer request that morning and how God answered it very blatantly.

Jenny, being the most gracious and kind and forgiving person I know, loved me in spite of this shocking news, and even thanked me for my honesty. Ugh. She asked if I would give it more prayer. I said I would pray about it, but that she should just plan on me not being there. It felt awful coming out of my mouth because it did not make me look very good. It made me look grumpy, fearful, pessimistic, and who knows what else; but, I said it because it was the truth. We prayed and I hung up feeling freer; my burdens were lifted. A funny thing happened after that... I was able to see the event with clearer eyes. I was no longer obligated to it. Because my fear was lifted and I was able to look at it objectively, I could pray into it without bitterness and unbelief. God opened my heart, and within 2 weeks I not only wanted to go, but my husband and children were helping to facilitate an environment so I could. In the end, I went. I did not cancel, and it was seriously the most honest event I had ever attended.

Johnson

Sorbe's honesty paired with being open to God brought about miraculous and life-altering things at that first speaking event. She obeyed, even though she was afraid. The way in which God interacted with Sorbe was so very personal. She wanted answers and He showed up at church with a specific message just for her. Hearing God's voice, moving past fear and obeying are key parts to this process of being open. Sorbe's interaction with God reminds me of two stories from my past.

This first story begins when I was a counselor at Camp Jim. I was leading my campers to the cafeteria for lunch. Right ahead of us was a large crowd and they were chanting something. I brought my campers closer to see what was going on. This crowd had encircled a very nervous young man. His hand shook as he looked fearfully at a huge black beetle wriggling on the surface of his palm. The crowd chanted, "Eat it! Eat it! Eat it! Don't be a baby, you can do it." It was easy to imagine being in this boy's shoes. I considered the horror of placing that gigantic insect into his mouth and hearing the sickening crunch as he took that first bite. It still makes my stomach churn just to imagine.

Amidst the crowd stood the camp pastor. He was speaking in a calm, clear voice that was easily distinguished from the mob. He said, "Paul, don't eat the beetle. Walk with me to lunch.

None of these kids would eat it, they just want to watch you. Paul, believe me, you don't want to eat that." The boy looked directly at the pastor and placed the beetle in his mouth. He chewed and chomped, gagging continuously, until he projectile vomited everywhere. The crowd was unsympathetic to the boy's embarrassment and pain. They simply moved on to lunch, many laughing at what they had just witnessed. The pastor remained. He walked over to the boy, placing a comforting hand on his shoulder. "Let's go find your Counselor and get you some new clothes. Paul, I would really like it if you would come and sit with me at lunch."

I love how even after the boy ate the beetle; the invitation was still there. What a beautiful picture of Jesus. It is so easy to look at this kid and think, "Well, I would never eat a bug, no matter how many people coerced me." There are many things in this life that are far worse than eating an insect. Anything we do that Jesus has told us not to is stupid, and there are always consequences for not obeying. Even if we have gone to the Beetle Buffet of Life, God is always standing by us, calling, whispering for us to follow Him. Please Holy Spirit, reveal the beetles in our lives. Open our ears to what you are saying and lead us to the places that you have set aside for us to go. Take a moment to pause here before we move to the next story. You can pray, write in your journal, maybe even get up and simply stretch.

Now that you have had a moment, let's move right into my next story.

Recently, God asked me to give a stranger a doughnut and it literally changed my life! I thought my weekend was all planned out and knew where His plans were guiding me...but what *He* had planned was actually a situation I desperately wanted to avoid. My plans were simple. I had a list of friends to meet with to encourage, fellowship with, love on, and surround myself in prayer with others. I love to minister to people, and I was positive that's what God was planning to do through me. Heading to a small town in Minnesota, I drove our 15-passenger van full of items in preparation to stage our home to go on the market. Truth be told, I was afraid to stay at my home alone, so I asked some family I had in town if I could stay at their house while they were away. They agreed and everything was set up for a productive work weekend with a side of Jesus. I assumed God had something amazing planned if I allowed Him, so I made a mental note to squeeze Him into my weekend.

Squeeze Him in?! He seriously took over all my plans...nothing went how I thought it should go! Staging the house with the help of friends took a little over an hour. One of my friends planning to help canceled and out of the blue someone else just happened to turn up and fill that spot. The replacement helper ended up needing a friend herself; and through our tears and openness, we were able to pray for hope and healing into her hurting heart. I was amazed! The weekend was going so much better than I had expected! Little did I know that God was building momentum to do something really big in my life.

Saturday, one of our prior youth group kids, now a young adult woman, dropped by for a visit. Her name was Amanda. The best way to describe Amanda is as a "hug from the Lord." People sometimes refer to her as Amanda Panda due to her gentle and loving nature! We planned on attending church together the next morning.

Two of my dear friends, Adam and Julia Weets, had recently started a new church plant in a coffee shop. I was so excited to see and attend their church, still blissfully unaware of what the Lord had in store for me. The service was incredibly encouraging, authentic, and undemanding. After the service we all socialized and ate doughnuts. I selected an adorable pink doughnut with rainbow sprinkles. Listen, I have a confession. I was *supposed* to be on a low carb diet with my mom and Sorbe. Doughnuts are a gateway to carb heaven or hell depending on your food choices. I indulged and took a bite; guilt immediately set in. Setting the pink, rainbow sprinkle doughnut back onto my plate, I stared at it and considered my options. I thought, "If I throw you away, that would be wasteful, and I hate wasting food. If I eat you doughnut, you will have won the war in my body to *not* eat you and I really don't want to lose to a pink doughnut." After much internal debate, I decided to keep the pastry on the plate held in my hand. I would neither eat it nor throw it away. I would simply hold onto it as I worked my way through the group, sharing in fellowship. Eventually, the church emptied, and my companions and I prepared to follow suit. With the doughnut still in hand we exited the building. Outside stood a woman, alone and staring up at the building next to where we stood. As soon as I saw her, I heard the Lord say, "Give her a doughnut." I looked down at my doughnut, shaking my head, and thought "God, I took a bite out of this doughnut. I am not going to offer her my gross, germy doughnut."

I walked right past her, and God insisted, in a kind yet authoritative voice, "Give her a doughnut." I still disagreed with God, because I could not understand why He would want me to give her *my* doughnut. I was so focused on the pink, rainbow sprinkled doughnut in my hand with the bite out of it that I wrestled with the idea that God wanted me to offer the woman my rejected pastry. Resolved to obey the God I love, I trusted He must have had a plan I could not foresee. I turned around, with my doughnut displayed for her to see and repeated the exact words the Lord told me to say. "Would you like a doughnut?" Immediately, her body relaxed, and a smile filled her face. She expressed how much she would love a doughnut. By the grace of God, Adam immediately offered to run back into the church for a fresh one. Relief washed over me. I was so thankful God was not intending for me to give the lady my doughnut and I relaxed comfortably into the moment, matching her smile. As

Adam turned to grab her a doughnut, she quickly asked, "Can my boyfriend have a doughnut?" Without seeing whom she was referring to, I joyfully replied, "Absolutely!"

She turned her head and beckoned for her boyfriend to join us. I was feeling fulfilled and happy to have connected with yet another surprise person in my Spirit-led-weekend, when I turned around and saw the man she had called over. My adrenaline surged. The man who rode up on his bicycle was Ben (whose name I've chosen to change for purposes of respect and privacy). Ben was my adopted girls' biological father! Fear swept over me in an instant; and unconsciously I quickly turned away from him. I had truly never wanted to run into that man again. The last time I saw him was prior to my girls' adoption. I had specifically stayed at a relative's house so that exact man wouldn't know where to find me. I was genuinely terrified of him. As the pastor and his wife engaged the couple in conversation, ignorant of this connection, I snuck over to Amanda and whispered, "That is the girls' biological father!"

Amanda's eyes widened, "Jenny, are you okay? Do you need to go back into the church?"

According to Amanda, I simply said, "No." In my memory of the moment, I thought I said something much more profound. What I was thinking was, "No. God tricked me with the doughnut. I am now obligated, being a 'semi-obedient' Christian, to stay here and see this play out."

Everything from that point on felt like it was happening in slow motion. Even though I didn't run away, I was trying to avoid the whole situation. I thought, "I will just look down and maybe he'll think I don't recognize him." The pastor and his wife had no idea what was going on and were continuing a casual getting-to-know-you conversation. They asked the couple's names and as Ben spoke his name loud enough for me to hear; I knew I couldn't hide anymore. I still didn't know what to do, so I silently and awkwardly approached Ben and stood in his personal bubble with my eyes closed. In my head, I asked God, "Okay, God, what do you want me to do?" God immediately responded. I heard, "pray for him." I opened my eyes, and said, "May I pray for you?" Ben agreed to my request right away. As I began praying, the words flowed from my mouth, and I felt a peace wash over me. Mid-sentence, I stopped and asked, "Ben, do you know who I am?" He said yes, and began to say such wonderful, kind, and loving things about my husband and myself. I can't remember the exact things that were spoken, but every word touched my heart and hit all of us like a powerful wave. Tears flowed from each of our eyes. It was truly an impossible, surreal moment in time. When he finished speaking, I said, "Ben, your girls pray for you. They pray that you will be set free from addiction, that you will find Jesus, and you will find a church."

I had never before called them *his girls*, as they are *my girls*, but in that moment, God opened up my heart to say it. Ben's shock over what was happening was painted on his face as he replied, "I have been feeling God calling me to go to church for months and with this whole crazy thing happening, I feel like he must have meant it."

From there things entered into a lighthearted conversation about the girls and their life. After a while, we went our separate ways. I went back into the church with my friends and proceeded to freak out. I just could not believe what God had just orchestrated for us to experience. It felt impossible to have experienced what God had accomplished in our lives through those mere minutes of obedience and openness to His plan!

Let me just say, God is genuinely smart. He knows us. He knew exactly what I could be faithful with—a doughnut. God knew what my response would have been if He had asked me to go back to that little town to meet the girls' biological father... "Nope. Not happening." Let's give me the benefit of the doubt and assume a scenario where I would have listened to that kind of urging from God. Would my loving, protective, not-crazy parents have agreed to watch my 6 children so I could go on such a seemingly foolhardy mission? The answer to this question is a resounding, "No!" Even if I had seen Ben from inside the coffee shop and God had ordered me to go and meet with him, I probably would have stalled–debating with God until the opportunity passed. Then I would have snapped my fingers and said, "Aw, shucks! Looks like I just missed him...maybe next time."

God had an amazing plan for me. He knew He could trust me with a doughnut. Did I initially trust it? Again, no. I questioned it. Why did I question? Because, God's plan seemed stupid. I could only see what was right in front of me; a rejected, pink, rainbow sprinkled, partially eaten doughnut.

The takeaway... and please do not miss this: *God has plans that are going to stretch you, mold you, and make you uncomfortable; but, His plans will produce a radically joyful life.* Most of us ask God for a life free of pain, a life of comfort. No one who was living for God in the Bible was called to a comfortable life; no adventure story ever revolves around the pursuit of complacent living. What would Jesus' life have looked like without suffering?[2] We would be lost without the redemptive work of Jesus on the Cross. God's way seems stupid but the God we serve is not limited by fear, doubt, or ability. He is a God that walks on stormy waters. He used mud to heal a blind man. He died to give us eternal life. He used a doughnut to encourage me to face my fears and to answer the prayers of my children for their biological father. If obeying God through the offering of a doughnut radically changed my life... Can you imagine what crazy, wondrous, uncomfortable, beautiful plans God has in store for you? Jesus spoke this in the words of the Lord's prayer, and he modeled it for us as the Trinity interacted in the garden before the cross when Jesus spoke with the Father, saying "Father, if You are willing, take this cup from Me. Yet not My will, but Yours be done" (Luke 22:42 NIV). These are words that will change the trajectory of your life if you choose to not only say them but apply them. God cares about and listens to our plans, but His plans will always be better than anything we could ever expect or imagine. I encourage you to turn around and take that step. Offer the doughnut.

Group Discussion Questions/Action Step/ Personal Reflection/Journal:

1. Be open with a friend or in your group. Share something vulnerable about your past, or a situation you are currently facing. Commit to pray together about it.

Assignment: What do you want to change? What action/obediece step can you take with Jesus today? Do that 1 thing and write down the results.

2. Be on the look out in your past, present, future for an opportunity to step into obedience with God. What is/was your donut moment? Pray for God to interrupt your day in powerful ways.

Prayer:

Dear Jesus,

Help me to be faithful with the doughnuts in my life. Holy Spirit please reveal things I am holding onto but need to share with others; trusting You to guide and direct my steps. Keep teaching me to perceive honesty as love. Make me brave. I trust you Lord, because Your plans are good.

In Jesus' Name, Amen.

5–FULLY OPEN

"But we have this treasure in jars of clay
to show that this all-surpassing power
is from God and not from us."
2 Corinthians 4:7 (NIV)

"Vulnerability is not knowing victory or defeat, its
understanding the necessity of both;
It's engaging. It's being all in."
Brene Brown, (Daring Greatly)

Sorbe

WHEN WE HOLD TIGHTLY TO SOMETHING,
WE ARE NOT LETTING IT GO.

To be fully open to the Lord means we are choosing to be vulnerable. We release (let go of) our *desire* for control to the Lord. In order for us to determine what we need to give to God; we must consider what we are holding on to. When we hold tightly to something, we are not letting it go. Not letting go reveals that we are not opening up to God. Fear is typically the driving factor behind our grip.

What does "taking control" look like for you? Let's discuss a few ways this *gripping* can manifest. Nearly all of us have a desire to manage our environment in some way or another. Would you agree? Imagine the following scenario. Your child is in the kitchen, and you've asked them to clean up after supper. You watch as they wipe the table, and the crumbs fall to the floor. They then proceed to load the dishwasher with chunks of food still on the plates. You notice the bowls sandwiched together too closely. There's no way those dishes will end up properly cleaned. Would you feel the urge to step in and take over the job? Or would you be the secret control person who waits until they leave the kitchen only to re-do everything they just did.

I want you to be honest with yourself and I promise not to point a crooked finger at you. Let's discuss and define some ways we find ourselves not allowing God in the driver's seat of our lives. We've discussed how to open ourselves up to God but many of us still find it difficult to trust Him. Often, it's because people in our lives have failed us and it can be hard not to assume God will fail us too. Things like relationships, our children, our time, our job, our finances, our health, and our futures can be areas where we find our biggest struggle. You may not even recognize that you are attempting to control these areas, so I will walk us through some scenarios.

Maybe you take control because you want things to go smoothly. You assume other people might screw it up; and, in order to prevent more work for yourself in the future you think, "It's better if I do it myself." However, because you only trust yourself to get the job done, you have a hard time delegating to others, ultimately leading to a heavier workload for yourself, defeating the plan of saving yourself more work.

Maybe your control presents itself through fear. People have let you down too many times! So, rather than opening yourself up to more disappointment, you don't ask for help anymore and just do things yourself.

What about falsely controlling your environment by turning off your feelings? You act as though nothing bothers you. Everything is just fine. You refuse to admit anything is wrong. You find yourself pushing your negative feelings deep down inside and imagine no one wants to hear what you think anyway. After all, others haven't in the past, so it's better to just be liked and act like it's all okay. Conflict is intimidating and you'd much rather do it yourself, so you don't have to deal with someone's irritation or backlash.

Are you a runner when things get tough or out of your control? Maybe quitting or leaving the situation is better than trying to work it out and you find yourself running away from your problems rather than sticking it out to find resolution.

Do any of these connect with how you might take control of situations in your life? Many of us feel the need to take control in order to prevent more work for ourselves, prevent a potential conflict, or spare ourselves from negative judgment. The question you must ask yourself is if it is truly *control* that you're taking? Or are you, in fact, a bit *out of control*?

The definition for control in the dictionary is *"not overly upset or excited: calm and able to think and act in a sensible way."*[1] For many of us, when we attempt to take control of a situation it is because we feel like things have stepped *out of our control*. We feel stressed, angry, frustrated, fearful, irritated, hopeless...we lose trust in others or ourselves, we quit, run away, overreact, shut down, close up, or over think...maybe we freeze up and cannot make a decision or we turn and engage like a caged animal. With any of these reactions to situations we find ourselves in, we think we are taking control, but we are revealing that we are out of control and God is not in the driver's seat. It's not the situation that is out of control, but us.

Believe me, I can relate to several forms of wanting to take control in one way or another. Friend, it's *our* opportunity to learn how to trust God in all situations and how to let go of *our* plans and open *our* hands up to God. Open. Vulnerable. Obedient.

BE RELENTLESS IN YOUR PRAYERS.

In God's Word, we are told to be anxious for nothing but pray about *everything*, with thankfulness in our hearts, and to give our requests to God so He can supply us with a peace beyond our understanding which ultimately guards our hearts and minds.[2] You may be asking, *"So what are we to do?! Not step in? Do nothing? Be doormats? Be passive?"* Not at all. In fact, quite the opposite! We are to be prayerful as we consider a more Christ-like response in every situation. This means seeking the Holy Spirit in prayer for his guidance and deliverance. Asking for wisdom. Receiving His comfort. Take whatever you're dealing with, hold nothing back, and say it all to Him in prayer. Repeat the process one hundred times if necessary. I once heard a pastor say, if you haven't received your answer or your breakthrough, then you're not done praying. Take this to heart. Be relentless in your prayers.

God gave us instructions on how to pray in Philippians 4:6-7. Turn to it in your Bible now and read the verse out loud if you would. These instructions guide us in dealing with stressful situations:

1. Be anxious for nothing.
2. Be thankful.
3. Bring our request to God.

And when we do those three things...

Jesus will give us peace beyond our understanding, which guards our hearts and minds!

In contrast, our humanness could lead us to:

1. Be fearful and anxious
2. Complain about how hard it all is and lose faith that anything will work out.
3. Try to fix it yourself.

And when we do those three things...

Stress continues.

I can tell you when I step in to *take control my way*, I often do it with the wrong attitude. Generally, I am frustrated, upset, or fearful. I might swear, throw my hands up in frustration, or go cry in the bedroom...either way, that is not God's way at all. He says in His Word that His yoke is easy, and His burden is light. He doesn't want that (stress) for us. When we take control, allowing our emotions to dictate our action, we choose to carry our own heavy burdens. Our way of dealing with these situations is, I'll say it again, **stupid**. Doing it our own way is a good way to hurt feelings, burn bridges, crush spirits, illicit anger, and create more work for ourselves. If we're being honest, taking control our way never brings peace. Not true (real) peace, anyway.

Johnson

This is so... relatable, Sorbe! This constant struggle between control and chaos is really exhausting. True peace sounds so refreshing. Excited to read more of what you are going to say about this issue of control.

Sorbe

In Psalm 37, we read that we are to commit our way to the Lord and trust Him and He will act. "He will bring forth your righteousness as the light, and your justice as the noonday" (Psalm 37:6 ESV). We are to be still before the Lord and wait patiently for Him.

Take a moment and look up these verses: Proverbs 3:5-8, Isaiah 40:31, Psalm 37:7-8, and Psalm 46:10. Please write them in the space below.

As you review these verses, do they sound more like the definition of control we see in the dictionary to you? *Calm, and able to think in a sensible way.* Some synonyms for the word *sensible* might be, *intelligent, logical, rational, sane, sober, wise, aware* and *discerning*. Those feel good. Some antonyms for sensible might be, *foolish, ignorant, impractical, irrational, stupid* or *unreasonable*. These feel less good.

IT'S NOT A GIVING-UP KIND OF WAITING.
IT'S AN EXPECTANT WAITING.

They will renew their strength, gain understanding, and discover straight paths. This form of waiting is active. It's not a giving-up kind of waiting. It's an expectant waiting; trusting in the character of God–that He is good. But waiting on God can feel tedious or tiresome...if we don't know (and trust) His character.

Circle back to some of the ways you've attempted to take charge. Now consider how you felt when you had to take charge. Did you experience peace? Was there thankfulness present in your heart? Was your strength renewed? Did you run without weariness? Or, like we discussed previously, were you fearful, frustrated, or stressed bearing the weight of a burden you were not meant to carry? So often we think that our way is best. We think, God's way takes time and effort and who's got time to wait? Why do we think this way? Again, I think it's because we don't trust God's character to truly come through in all circumstances. It's the same reason we take control from other people, too. We don't truly believe they have our best interests at heart. And maybe they don't... but God does.

Let me clarify something about the character of God concerning control. He IS sovereign; but He gives us free will. That free will allows us to choose how we will think, believe, and act. I love how C.S. Lewis expounds on it. "God created things which had free will. That means creatures which can go either wrong or right...If a thing is free to be good it's also free to be bad. And free will is what has made evil possible. Why, then, did God give them free will? Because free will, though it makes evil possible, is also the only thing that makes possible any love or goodness or joy worth having."[3] God is good, and the devil is not. Sin and brokenness are evident on this earth and God has given *us*, (His [saved] people, His Saints), the ability to stand in stark contrast to evil by doing things His way instead of our own (stupid) way. Would you agree that oftentimes we have our own interests at heart? I would. I may not be intending to be selfish, but when I "take control", that is exactly how I am behaving... Selfish, self-preserving, fearful, prideful, etc. Ugh. Don't worry, I'm walking this road right along with you. Fear not, there is hope! Look at what is written in Jeremiah 29:11, "For I know the plans I have for you[...] plans to prosper and not harm you, plans to give you a hope and a future." Giving us a hope and a future really sounds like He's on our side. Are you willing to grab hold of this promise? The Lord is intentional about it, but we must choose to do things God's way to receive the promised blessings and that's not always easy. We must change our habits and choose to both perceive and trust the true character of God.

Friend, you can call out to God when you are feeling out of control. You can learn to let go and let God, meaning releasing your grasp. Look down at your hand right now. Either hand or both hands if you'd like. Open them and take a nice deep breath. As you do this, confess to Jesus your fears, frustration, and anger concerning a particular situation that comes to mind. I like to envision myself laying them at the foot of the cross when I pray. I apply all that we receive from what Christ did on that cross over my situation.

ALLOWING OUR EMOTIONS TO REIGN OVER TRUTH LEADS TO CHAOS AND DESTRUCTION IN OUR THOUGHTS AND OUTSIDE RELATIONSHIPS.

So why do things feel out of control to us then? Did you catch that? "Feel" out of control. The question is, are things truly out of control, or do we just feel that they are? Feelings are an indicator of what we believe to be true, but not necessarily what is true. Feelings can deceive us and if we give them the right to reign, they will take charge over our reactions. Allowing our emotions to reign over truth leads to chaos and destruction in our thoughts and our outside relationships.

"Jesus said, 'I was born a King, and I have come into this world to prove what truth really is. And everyone who loves the truth will receive my words.'"

John 18:37 (TPT)

We have a saying in our home: "Think before you act." No doubt you've heard that before. We have two boys. Our youngest is naturally more emotional. Because of this, he can be reactive and impulsive. He can get offended, and experience hurt feelings more easily. He can also be very empathetic and considerate. He notices other kids who may be hurting and will seek them out. This more emotional character can bring vibrancy and excitement into his life, but when unstable it can also bring hardship and brokenness. Because of his more sensitive nature, I knew he could be more of a target to internet predators. But both of my boys would need skills and knowledge in order to navigate this world of good and evil.

Knowing the pressures and the lure of pornography that determined to lure them into addiction, I purchased several books teaching them how to say NO to it. I knew they would need to learn the skills *before* they encountered their first image. Based on what I was reading regarding how many kids see pornography by the age of 10, I knew it would not be *IF* they were exposed, but a *WHEN*. These books[4] trained my kids in the steps to take when they see porn on the internet. For example, if an image comes up on the screen that is inappropriate, they were taught that they have both the power and the choice to look away, close the game, and go tell mom or dad about it. By making the right choice, they learned it will prevent future harm to their minds, their bodies, and their future relationships.

My boys learned they are in control of how they react to the situations that come at them unexpectedly. The image or situation is not in charge; rather, they are. We had many discussions along the way, to practice what they would do if and when...and they became empowered, which placed them in control–the right kind of control. Evil was out there, and they needed to know what to do when it showed its ugly face. Why would this be relevant to our discussion of control? Because we know that in our own lives, we have stressful situations that show up unexpectedly. Just like an inappropriate pop-up on one of my boys' games, we all need to have the knowledge, understanding and a plan in place to know what to do when these situations arise. More than that, we need the wisdom to implement those skills in time of need. This is maturity. My boys are now more prepared for what will inevitably come their way. Being prepared in advance for stressful situations helps protect us, not only now, but in our future.

Let's talk about the brain quickly. I remember reading something a while back about our thinking brain versus our emotional brain. Say you see an ice cream truck across the street... Knowing what is being sold from that truck, you begin to desire what's in it. In that moment, your emotional brain tells you to run over to that truck. Your thinking brain, however, tells you to look both ways before you cross the road. If your emotional brain was in charge and you impulsively ran over to that truck parked across the street, there's a chance that you could get hit by a car. That's a great analogy for kids, but how about we make this story a little more applicable for us adults. Imagine you're on a diet. You've decided to take a break from sugar for one month. It's been going well so far...three days down and you're feeling fairly successful. You need to take your daughter to a birthday party. You smell freshly baked cake, and the ice cream has been set out. Plates of cake and ice cream are now out on the table and your stomach begins to rumble. Your emotional brain starts working overtime. I bet you already know what your brain would be saying. "It's only one piece. No big deal." "I'll just start the diet again on Monday." If you allow those thoughts to overtake your brain, pretty soon you will have a very hard time sticking to your diet. You're allowing your emotional brain to have power over you. But, if you have prepared ahead of time for this, your thinking brain is ready for the temptation. Your thinking brain would have told you to eat before you went to the party. Maybe you would have packed yourself a sugar free snack just in case. In both scenarios your emotional and thinking brain went with you, but in the first scenario you gave your emotional brain all the power and, in the end, you would have likely given in to the temptation. By doing so, you would have failed the plan you set for yourself and often shame and guilt are sure to follow. However, in the second scenario, you put your thinking brain in the driver's seat. You prepared yourself for the temptation, ultimately giving it no power over you, thus leading to a feeling of success and ultimately a feeling of being in control. Your environment did not own you.

So often, we do stupid things because we are only using our emotional brain. I want you to take a moment, if you will, to think of the times where you allowed your emotional brain to be in control. How did it affect your situation? Did it cause you to overreact, maybe act impulsively, only later to regret that decision? Did you say something you didn't mean in the heat of the moment? Emotions and thinking–we need them both. But better yet, we need them both submitted and surrendered to God. Do you know what God has given us believers? The mind of Christ. "For who has known the mind and purposes of the Lord, so as to instruct him? But we have the mind of Christ to be guided by His thoughts and purposes" (1 Corinthians 2:16 AMP). Woah. That's awesome. We have the mind of Christ. You may be thinking, 'I sure don't act like I have the mind of Christ.' If you are a born-again, Jesus-loving believer, you absolutely have the mind of Christ. However, you can have something and not know how to utilize it.

On the previous page you wrote down my life verse, Proverbs 3:5-8. If I trust in the Lord with *all* my heart and *do not* lean on my own understanding, but in all my ways, submit my will (and my emotions) to Him... He will make my paths straight before me. My mother used to sing this verse to me when I found myself in situations where I was unsure how to proceed. It has consistently helped me shift from a perspective of fear, doubt, and worry, to setting my focus on Christ. It's the *truth-over-my-emotions* plan that when I choose to apply it to my situation, I can trust God will show me the correct course on which to tread.

> *"Commit your work to the Lord, and your plans will be established."*
>
> Proverbs 16:3 (NIV)

> *"Commit your way to the Lord; trust in Him, and He will act....Be not wise in your own eyes; fear the Lord and turn away from evil. It will be healing to your flesh and refreshment to your bones."*
>
> Psalm 37:5,7 (ESV)

What outcomes do you see listed in the above instructions if we do it God's way instead of our (stupid) way? Grab a highlighter if you will and highlight the blessing that comes with doing it God's way. Ponder that outcome for a moment. Brings hope, doesn't it? It sure does to me because my way was not working so well.

This is how the Word of God operates, it's an instruction manual. It lists the issue or problem, then tells us how to deal with our issue, following up with the blessing we receive when we do it God's way. Remember how I mentioned how we have three parts? A body, a soul, and a spirit. This is another area where we must teach our soul to submit to the Spirit (where the Holy Spirit resides) rather than the body (our will). God's truth in scripture, applied to our lives, is how we win the battle over our way of living stupid.

Some of you didn't relate to those other versions of control. Maybe you are not an emotional person, and you would consider yourself to be quite level-headed. This would be how our eldest son would describe himself. This son is a big thinker. He assesses risk and cost continually. He thinks deeply and logically. For a while, his process of thought kept him from venturing into new things. You could call it fear of risk. *What if I fail? What if I get hurt? What if it doesn't deliver what it promises?* For him, I began to speak a new motto–one I knew he wouldn't take too far. One that would allow himself to consider whether he was attempting to control all outcomes, thereby keeping himself from moving forward. "Don't think, just do." He was aware I was cautioning his brother to *think before you act*. He observed how making impulsive decisions got his brother into trouble and he did not want that life. Safety and thought were *his* way to control his environment. The trouble was, it was keeping him from stretching his faith and learning how to rely on the Lord. Let me share a story.

We put him in swimming lessons. All was well enough until it came time for him to jump into the water into the arms of the lifeguard beneath the low diving board. All the safety measures needed for this level up training exercise were in place: The trained lifeguard, the floaty in her hand for him to grab onto when he landed, and a life jacket strapped on his body. I observed him from the side of the pool, standing at the end of the board, looking down at the lifeguard beckoning him to jump. He wouldn't do it. I could imagine his racing thoughts–the what-ifs. Year three of lessons, and here we were again with the what-ifs rearing their ugly heads. To him, the jump off the diving board posed too great a risk. What if the lifeguard doesn't catch me? What if I get water up my nose? What if I can't swim as well as they say I can? What if I drown? Can you sense the mental spiral? What our son thought was logical reasoning was in fact him submitting his mind to irrational fear. You see, what-ifs are a form of control, too. *If I do this, then that negative consequence will happen to me.* So, the best choice for him became, "I just won't do it." Fear won over and over. And it was stealing advancement, new opportunities, and faith rooted in trust, from him.

Who needs adventure anyway? Over and over, I would hear him make rationalizations for his decision to avoid risk, even low-risk activities. This was going to be a problem for him in the future if left unaddressed. Honestly, it was a problem for him now. Where was seeking and trusting the Lord in his life? He'd maybe say a quick prayer, but it wouldn't have mattered what God was saying because he wasn't going to do it anyway. I could no longer stand passively by and allow him to submit to fear that I knew would ultimately keep him from greater blessings.

I decided to act and join him where he stood on that diving board. I saw his little body trembling at the end of it, his face realizing what I had come to do. He knew I was going to 'help' him off the diving board. Gently, I lifted him off his feet and lowered him into the water to the sweet and very capable lifeguard below. He barely got wet. He was mad at me, indignant that I would overthrow his choice. Well, I loved him too much to let him stay there. Fear had stolen from him enough, and if he wouldn't deal with it, I would.

Later that same summer we were at that same pool. He saw kids going down these cool waterslides and started to desire more adventure than the baby area. *Thank you, Jesus, he is stretching.* But there it was again, fear and the need to control his environment. What if I get stuck? What if there's too much water on the slide and I drown? What if it goes too fast for me? On and on these thoughts were building. No amount of my logical reasoning was outweighing his fears. "Look at that little kid that just went up there. Look, they're laughing! They're having fun! Oh, they're going again. You can do this! I believe in you!" But a war was raging in his mind and soul. On one side, his desire for more adventure was growing; but on the other, old habits and a familiar spirit–fear–were trying to persuade him the risk was too great. Yet, I was beginning to witness his desire for *more,* dismantling the debilitating fear. *Please Lord,* I prayed desperately, *let his desire for adventure win. Show him he CAN do these things. Do not allow this fear to swallow him and steal the greater blessing again.* After what seemed like hours of him pacing and discussing with himself and me all the positive outcomes of taking this risk, trying to talk himself into doing it, he finally declared he would walk up there. As you all now know, I was in the military. I know what the mind is capable of accomplishing and I allowed him to go up there without me shadowing him. It would be his decision. Well, mostly. Another battle in his mind ensued once he sat down on that slide. I was below, silently cheering him on and praying. *Come on buddy! You're safe! I'm here. You will love this! You will gain so much confidence! Just do it.* But I saw what I had seen so many times before. *What if...* Oh, but Jesus was all over this moment and I had a partner I wasn't originally aware of... someone who would help me, help him. No one else was up there. It was just him, the young lifeguard, and his thoughts. I don't know if that sweet girl had seen him oscillating all day or if she had just worked this spot long enough that she'd seen this fear in kids before. She looked down at me and I gave her the body language message to use her foot to gently push him down the slide.

Okay, before you judge me here, I have watched my child since he could walk, hide behind fear. Fear is a liar. It is a thief. I saw great and lovely things in my son, and he was not living his full potential. Not *my* full potential for him, mind you... *His* full potential. That sweet and brave lifeguard nodded in understanding to my unspoken message, flashing me a worried smile whilst she ever so gently began to apply pressure to his back until he had no choice but to let go and, well, enjoy the ride. I braced myself for the potential recompense of anger that he has shown me before, but I am telling you, my heart was swelling with love for him. I loved him so much that I could not allow fear to win in his life again. Out he popped, off the slide and into the water. He easily swam to the steps and stepped out to face me. My heart was pounding out of my chest. *Did I go too far this time?* I bore a consoling smile on my face as he approached; bracing myself for whatever came next. Like I mentioned earlier, he is not emotionally driven, he leads with logic. He's also no liar and doesn't try to manipulate with pretense or false emotion. Standing before me I saw a smile begin to emerge from his lips and reach into his eyes. "How was it, buddy?" I marveled. "It was really great, mom." Pride flooded my heart, and I sent a silent cry of thanksgiving and gratitude to the Lord. "Will you go again?" "Yes, I will." I lost count of how many times he went down that slide. Fear lost its hold on my boy that day. Yes, he needed a nudge. *We* sometimes do, don't we? But he made the choice to face his fear and step into adventure and he was blessed for it. (I was blessed for it!) For our son, that day marked the beginning of a new perspective. He began to realize that fear was just a thing that he could *allow* to win, or he could *choose* to overcome it by stepping into faith.

In the book of Matthew, chapter 21, the disciples watch Jesus curse a fig tree and see it immediately wither. As shocking as seeing that plant respond to Jesus' words was, so were the words that Jesus spoke to them right after that. "Truly, I say to you, if you have faith and do not doubt, you will not only do what has been done to the fig tree, but even if you say to this mountain, 'Be taken up and thrown into the sea,' it will happen. And whatever you ask in prayer, you will receive, if you have faith." This is the kind of faith I want my sons to have, that *I* want to have, and I want you to have too.

Johnson

> *"Then you will cry out on that day because of your king whom you have chosen for yourselves, but the Lord will not answer you on that day [because you have rejected Him as King]." Nevertheless, the people refused to listen to the voice of Samuel, and they said, "No, but there shall be a king over us, so that we too may be like all the nations [around us], that our king may judge [and govern] us and go out before us and fight our battles."*
>
> 1 Samuel 8:18-20 (AMP)

Whose voice are you listening to? Who or what is the reigning authority over your body, heart, and mind? Do you know how to listen to God? These are some of the questions we will be working through in this next section. But first, for your enjoyment, let's look at another epic example of stupid from the Bible. We are going to dig into 1 Samuel 8:1-21. I will give you a summary here, but feel free to go deeper and read through it on your own. In fact, I highly recommend you do that—the endeavor is worth the undertaking.

Israel was tired of being different. They wanted a king to rule over them. God had specifically called[5] this nation–they were chosen for a grand purpose–but instead they longed to imitate those around them. God's chosen people plead with Samuel to approach Him for a king other than the Lord, *their* God[6]. They desired to be led by a human king; one they could see, touch and experience tangibly on earth. Samuel kept a close relationship with God ever since he was a little boy. He immediately took their request before the Lord. God knew what His people were really saying, "God, we don't trust you. We no longer want you to lead us. We want an earthly government, a king, a human being to rule over us. We want to be like everyone else. But God, don't feel too bad, we will let you pick your replacement. We still want you to bless us, even though we don't think you are really good enough."

Ouch! What a painful, horrific thing to say to God! How did the Creator of the universe respond? In response to their request, the Lord provided Samuel with a detailed list, clearly stating the depth of how stupid their request was for a King. Basically, a pointed warning filled with all the bad things an earthly ruler would bring to Israel. There was not a single positive thing on His list–zero, zilch, nada! God revealed the depth of how stupid their request was to His prophet. I picture Samuel nodding his head in understanding, certain that the people would listen to God's truth and change their minds. Nope. Samuel speaks, tells them everything, and they still want their earthly king. What?! Are you kidding me...did I miss something?! At what point in this long list of dire warnings did they decide that a king would be a good idea? The truth is, they were hearing but not listening. They didn't care what God had to say. So, the Lord gave them what they thought they wanted–an earthly king. Their decision ultimately led Israel to be taken over by other nations. This simple deviation to do things their own way caused them and future generations to suffer unimaginable pain and disconnect from the Lord. Imperfect human people were never meant to replace a perfect and Holy God. In between the Old and New Testaments, many scholars believe that God went silent. Silent for around 400 years.[7] I really want to make this funny for you, to lighten the mood, but it simply isn't possible. This truly is as awful and depressing as it sounds.

I think we need to just sit here a minute. What if God had left us there, hopelessly lost, left to do things our own way? This is not the freedom the world claims it to be! It is dying and embracing the void. It is pain with no hope of healing. This is nihilism–a life devoid of purpose and meaning. *Death*...in the truest sense of the word. Have you and I been living in this place? Are we listening to God or choosing to live in a world where He is silent?

> *"He has caused us to be born again to a living hope through the resurrection of Jesus Christ from the dead, to an inheritance that is imperishable, undefiled, and unfading, kept in heaven for you."*
>
> 1 Peter 1:3-4 (ESV)

> *"But the Helper, the Holy Spirit, whom the Father will send in my name, will teach you all things and remind you of everything that I have told you."*
>
> John 14:26 (ESV)

> "My sheep listen to my voice; I know them, and they follow me. I give them eternal life, and they shall never perish; no one will snatch them out of my hand. My Father, who *has given them to me, is greater than all; no one can snatch them out of my Father's hand. I and the Father are one."*
>
> John 10:27-30 (NIV)

Time to pray. Heavenly Father, we invite your Holy Spirit into this conversation. We know the enemy intends to deliberately keep us from hearing your voice. Lord, we desire intimacy with you. Teach us how to listen. Help us to walk with you, all the days of our life. We ask all these things in the precious name of your son, Jesus.

To understand when the Lord is speaking, we need to know how His voice sounds. Here is a test...Is this God or the enemy speaking? During the peak of one of the darkest moments in my life, I heard a whisper. "You are broken. You are too tired to fight anymore. Give up. What benefit has "giving everything" done for you? It has destroyed you. You are alone. You will never have peace. I know how to hurt you, and more is coming. You are not strong enough to fight anymore. You cannot even get out of bed this morning! Your children are dying, and you cannot help them. You will watch your house burn before your eyes." I can literally hear the hiss of the serpent in these words as I relay them to you. Yep, this was the enemy. This was 100% not Jesus. But what *does* God sound like? In what ways does He speak to us? How can we tell the difference?

Sorbe

You can see the words spoken to Johnson above were not life-bringing words, but those of death. I am NOT okay with verbal threats from an invisible enemy. You and I want to live the abundant life Jesus promised us in John 10:10, believe me. *Please* get yourself a notebook right now, or even write in the margins on this page! List all the lies you have heard spoken over you. We are going to nuke those lies and send them straight to hell where they belong.

> *"We know that the word of God is living and active, sharper than any two-edged sword, piercing to the division of soul and of spirit, of joints and of marrow, and discerning the thoughts and intentions of the heart."*
>
> Hebrews 4:12 (ESV)

Johnson

Discerning the difference between God's voice and the devil's is a crucial part of our decision to be 'Open' to the Lord. In the following sections, you will learn how to confront the lies the enemy throws your way. The Bible is our instruction manual, and it is what He has given us to combat these destructive demonic words. Let's begin...

You are broken...

"And you are complete in Him, who is the head of all principality and power." Colossians 2:10 (NKJV)

"And let steadfastness have its full effect, that you may be perfect and complete, lacking in nothing." James 1:4 (ESV)

"He heals the brokenhearted and binds up their wounds." Psalm 147:3 (NIV)

These three verses directly come against the lie that "I am broken". Do you see the power of scripture?! Take a minute and read those above verses again. Can these words from God combat any of the lies you jotted in your margins? Yes, unequivocally. These scriptures are our heavenly weapons of warfare; our firm foundation from which we stand. Now, let's move on through the rest of these examples.

You are too tired to fight anymore...

"If your faith remains strong, even while surrounded by life's difficulties, you will continue to experience the untold blessings of God! True happiness comes as you pass the test with faith, and receive the victorious crown of life promised to every lover of God!" James 1:12 (TPT)

"I have learned the secret of being filled and going hungry, both of having abundance and suffering need. I can do ***all*** *things* ***through Him*** who strengthens me." Philippians 4:12b-13 (NASB) (Emphasis mine)

"He gives strength to the weary and increases the power of the weak. Even youths grow tired and weary, and young men stumble and fall; but those who hope in the Lord will renew their strength. They will soar on wings like eagles; they will run and not grow weary; they will walk and not be faint." Isaiah 40:29-31 (NIV)

"Do not fear, for I am with you; do not anxiously look about you, for I am your God. I will strengthen you, surely I will help you, surely I will uphold you with My righteous right hand." Isaiah 41:10 (NASB)

Give up. What benefit has "giving everything" done for you?

"And whatever you do, in word or deed, do everything in the name of the Lord Jesus, giving thanks to God the Father through Him." Colossians 3:17 (ESV)

"Let us not become weary in doing good, for at the proper time we will reap a harvest if we do not give up." Galatians 6:9 (NIV)

And we know that for those who love God all things work together for good, for those who are called according to His purpose. Romans 8:28 (ESV)

You will never have peace...

Peace I leave with you; my peace I give you. I do not give to you as the world gives. Do not let your hearts be troubled and do not be afraid. John 14:27 (NIV)

The Lord is my shepherd; I have all that I need. He lets me rest in green meadows; he leads me beside peaceful streams. He renews my strength. Psalm 23:1-3 (NLT)

Even when I walk through the darkest valley, I will not be afraid, for you are close beside me. Your rod and your staff protect and comfort me. Psalm 23:4 (NLT)

You are alone...

Then Jesus came to them and said, "*All authority* in heaven and on earth has been given to me. Therefore go and make disciples of all nations, baptizing them in the name of the Father and of the Son and of the Holy Spirit, and teaching them to obey everything I have commanded you. And surely *I am with you always*, to the very end of the age." Matthew 28:18-20 (NIV) (Emphasis mine)

So be strong and courageous! Do not be afraid and do not panic before them. For the Lord your God will personally go ahead of you. He will neither fail you nor abandon you." Deuteronomy 31:6 (NLT)

Whoever dwells in the shelter of the Most High will rest in the shadow of the Almighty. I will say of the Lord, "He is my refuge and my fortress, my God, in whom I trust." Psalm 91:1-2 (NIV)

I know how to hurt you, and more is coming...

Trust in the Lord with all your heart and lean not unto your own understanding. In all your ways acknowledge Him and He shall direct your paths. Proverbs 3:5-6 (KJ 2000)

You will not fear the terror of night, nor the arrow that flies by day, nor the pestilence that stalks in the darkness, nor the plague that destroys at midday. Psalm 91:5-6 (NIV) (Emphasis mine)

Even when I walk through the darkest valley, I will not be afraid, for you are close beside me. Your rod and your staff protect and comfort me. Psalm 23:4 (NLT)

Your children are dying, and you cannot help them. You will watch your house burn before your eyes...

> "'For I,' declares the Lord, 'will be a wall of fire around her [protecting her from enemies], and I will be the glory in her midst.'" Zechariah 2:5 (AMP)

> And the devil that deceived them was cast into the lake of fire and sulfur, where the beast and the false prophet [were cast] and shall be tormented day and night forever and ever. Revelations 20:10 (NMV)

> John answered them all, saying, "I baptize you with water, but he who is mightier than I is coming, the strap of whose sandals I am not worthy to untie. He will baptize you with the Holy Spirit *and* fire." Luke 3:16 (ESV) (Emphasis mine)

Can you hear and see the difference? Are you looking for encouragement? Are you looking for a reason to keep on living? Do you long for more than what this world has to offer you? I can promise you this, when you are open to inviting God into your daily life, you will find that your life begins to change for the better.

Sorbe

When God created us, He created us in His image intentionally. Just as God, Jesus, and the Holy Spirit are one, we too are made of three parts: our Body, our Soul, and our Spirit. Because Adam sinned in the garden, all generations after him were born into sin. This is where the Lord brought salvation into His plan. We need to be saved from our sin. And that's why Jesus came to earth. He set His deity aside to become like us humans. Wow.

> *Though he was God, he did not think of equality with God as something to cling to. Instead, he gave up his divine*

privileges; he took the humble position of a slave and was born as a human being. When he appeared in human form, he humbled himself in obedience to God and died a criminal's death on a cross.

Philippians 2:6-8 (NLT)

Except, unlike all of us, Jesus lived a sinless life. His life paid the debt for the consequence of sin. For those of us who realize our sinfulness, and that the ultimate consequence of sin is death and hell, we *need* a Savior*. (*Savior. Noun. One who saves, rescues, delivers, or redeems from danger, death, or destruction; a deliverer; a redeemer. Jesus.)

"For the wages of sin is death, but the free gift of God is eternal life through Christ Jesus our Lord."

Romans 6:23 (NLT)

If we are guilty of sin (we all are), we do not qualify in saving ourselves and require a savior. Our attempt to be good enough in hopes of getting to heaven will not cut it. We have all sinned and our sin (apart from salvation) separates us from God. Spiritual Death is the consequence for sin, period. Jesus is the only one qualified to be our Savior from the death penalty and we need to be <u>reborn</u>! If you've not heard this term before, you are not alone. Let's read the communication between Jesus and Nicodemus, who also didn't get it at first.

"Jesus replied, "I tell you the truth, unless you are <u>born again</u>, you cannot see the Kingdom of God." "What do you mean?" exclaimed Nicodemus. "How can an old man go back into his mother's womb and be born again?" Jesus replied, "<u>I assure you, no one can enter the Kingdom of God without being born of water and the Spirit. Humans</u>

can reproduce only human life, but the Holy Spirit gives birth to spiritual life...."For this is how God loved the world: He gave his one and only Son, so that everyone who believes in him will not perish but have eternal life. God sent his Son into the world not to judge the world, but to save the world through him."

John 3:3-6; 16-17 (NLT*)*

Your spiritual rebirth through faith in Jesus is how the transformation truly begins, it gives you two things you will never again want to live without, a heavenly seal, and a new title of, a child of God. Think of it as adoption into a completely new lineage; a heavenly one!

"Therefore if anyone is in Christ [that is, grafted in, joined to Him by faith in Him as Savior], he is a new creature [reborn and renewed by the Holy Spirit]; the old things [the previous moral and spiritual condition] have passed away. Behold, new things have come [because spiritual awakening brings a new life.]"

2 Corinthians 5:17 (AMP)

The Holy Spirit of God comes to live in our Spirit when we acknowledge that Jesus Christ's sacrifice was to pay the open debt of [our] sin needing to be paid. It's a free gift for us to accept and one that should humble us to the core because **it's all about love**. Jesus loves us so very much. He's inviting us to be forgiven and saved. We have the choice to either accept the open invitation or deny it. If we accept it, our Spirit is filled to the brim... full of the power of heaven through Christ and the Holy Spirit! If we deny the invitation, our Spirit is empty and vulnerable to the brokenness of the world that will prevent us from eternal life in Heaven with the One who loved us first. Don't wait. Invite Him in. You will no longer be empty.

To have all things through Christ who gives us strength, we need to accept Jesus as our Lord and savior. We must invite Him to come in and *have His way in us*. Jesus will not force His way in; nor will you get saved by going to church, graduating from confirmation, being baptized or any other religious practice. These practices are good, but without a personal relationship with Christ they are empty. We are ultimately lost without Him. Not everyone who calls out to Jesus will enter the Kingdom of Heaven (see verse below). Even people who look church-like will not automatically be allowed in just because they looked good or talked the talk. In Matthew 7:21-24, we read that only those who do the will of God in heaven will enter. It's a heart issue.

> *"Not everyone who says to me, 'Lord, Lord,' will enter the kingdom of heaven, but only the one who does the will of my Father who is in heaven. Many will say to me on that day, 'Lord, Lord, did we not prophesy in your name and in your name drive out demons and in your name perform many miracles?' Then I will tell them plainly, 'I never knew you. Away from me, you evildoers!'*
>
> Matthew 7:21-24 (NIV)

Don't let this passage scare you. Allow it to open your eyes to see that religious acts, traditions, or simply believing Jesus and God are real are not enough. Those acts and ideologies do not pay the penalty for sin when they stand alone. It is by believing and accepting Jesus as Lord in your life. Without Him directing our lives, we don't stand a chance at the gates of heaven. Romans 6:23 (NLT) says, "For the wages of sin is *death*, but the free gift of God is eternal *life* in Christ Jesus our Lord." *Nothing we do ourselves can save us*. We must acknowledge that the sacrifice

Jesus made for us is the only thing which truly matters. Our relationship with Him is what brings us freedom.

Johnson

> *Jesus said to him, "I am the way, and the truth, and the life. No one comes to the Father except through Me."*
>
> John 14:6 (ESV)

We must be born again. Right now, you can invite Jesus into your life. How amazing is that?! Go for it. Right now. Don't wait for the perfect moment–*this is* the perfect moment. Accept and ask Jesus Christ into your life and step into salvation with both feet. Jesus will accept you and make you His child no matter what resides in your past. He *wants* to renew you, free you, and strengthen you!

> *But to all who did receive Him, who believed in His name, He gave the right to become children of God, who were born, not of blood nor of the will of the flesh nor of the will of man, but of God.*
>
> John 1:12-13 (ESV)

In other words, we get reborn. Not through our mommas, but spiritually reborn. We receive and believe, and God gives us the right to be called His child! We become a son or daughter of God! What an awesome inheritance and title.

Let me show you how to use scripture to pray. What you are about to recite comes directly from God's Word. Pray it out loud. You can get on your knees if you want. You can say it wherever you are or call a friend to pray it together. This is a very special moment that you will never forget!

> *"If you declare with your mouth, "Jesus is Lord," and believe in your heart that God raised him from the dead, **you will be saved**. For it is **with your heart** that you believe and are justified, and it is **with your mouth** that you profess your faith and are saved. As Scripture says, "Anyone who believes in him will never be put to shame."*
>
> Romans 10:9-11 (NIV) (Emphasis mine)

Prayer:

"Lord, I choose you! I believe that you came to earth to save me from the consequences of my sin, and I want your salvation! I ask You to forgive me for my sinful ways and thoughts and I forgive myself. I receive your forgiveness right now. I am forgiven. I cancel all of satan's authority over me by the power of Jesus's name and by the blood He shed on the cross for my sins. My Father, my God–I am now yours and You are mine. I renounce and repent for my old and sinful ways and take on Your ways. I receive this new life, a forgiven life. Fill me now with your Holy Spirit. Teach me your ways and give me understanding. Holy Spirit, reveal to me my new identity in Jesus Christ. In Jesus' Name, Amen."

Sorbe

If you have invited Jesus into your life, WELCOME to the Family!! You are a New Creation! You have been made new! This is where you were always meant to be. Know that what you just did gave you a new heavenly heritage and a new spiritual family. Tell a friend. And keep on praying

A note for believers: Please feel free to go back up and read through the message and verses above. Have you ever struggled to share the Gospel to someone? There are so many people hurting and needing a Savior; and you may very well be the one to bring them this much needed answer. Take a moment and pray with us for those who are at a crossroads right now. Pray they will not put this book down, but instead make the decision to become a child of God.

Group Discussion Questions/Action Step/ Personal Reflection/Journal:

- Are you more of an emotionally-brained or thinking-brained person? What is your way of taking control?

- In Sorbe's story about her son and the water, she shared how her son needed help moving past his fear. In what ways do you sense God nudging you?

- Who or what has been your earthly king? What things do you put above God? Consider your horoscope, social media, your phone, the news, safety, fears, good or bad relationships, Google, self-help books...

Assignment: In the margins, write out a lie you have believed. Find a scripture that contrasts it, like Johnson did above. Write it out below the lie. Why stop with one? Do as many as you like.

Prayer:

Dear Jesus,

Thank you for dying on that cross for my sins. You even did it willingly. You love me so much. Please teach me more about Your love. Help me to receive Your love so that I can love others like You do. Holy Spirit, teach me how to tap into Your power so that I can live a victorious life. I have been forgiven and set free. Praise Your Holy Name!

In Jesus' name I pray. Amen

TRUST THE PROCESS

We were getting stronger, both mentally and physically, becoming more resilient and meshing as a team. If ever our bodies failed us, we had our battle buddies next to us, picking us up and keeping us moving. Quitting was not an option. Obedience was always expected. Obey, don't think, just do. Trust. Do. Never quit. This was a very important lesson in my life.
Sorbe

Trust in and rely confidently on the Lord with all your heart and do not rely on your own insight or understanding. In all your ways know and acknowledge and recognize Him, And He will make your paths straight and smooth [removing obstacles that block your way]. Do not be wise in your own eyes; Fear the Lord [with reverent awe and obedience] and turn [entirely] away from evil. It will be health to your body [your marrow, your nerves, your sinews, your muscles—all your inner parts] and refreshment (physical well-being) to your bones.
Proverbs 3:5-8 (AMP)

Trust: noun
1: firm belief in the reliability, truth, ability, or strength of someone or something.

"Relations have to be built on trust."

6–TRUST–HE IS GOOD (ACTIVE NOT PASSIVE)

"Obey the Word of God. If you hear only and do not act, you are only fooling yourself. Anyone who hears the Word of God and does not obey is like a man looking at his face in a mirror. After he sees himself and goes away, he forgets what he looks like. But the one who keeps looking into God's perfect Law and does not forget it will do what it says and be happy as he does it. God's Word makes men free."
James 1:22-25 (NLT)

"Waiting on God is not laziness. Waiting on God is not going to sleep. Waiting on God is not the abandonment of effort. Waiting on God means, first, activity under command; second, readiness for any new command that may come; third, the ability to do nothing until the command is given."
J.I.Packer

Johnson

Being *open* to the Lord is much simpler when compared to *trusting the process*, which can be more of an emotional roller coaster. Being *open* is like buckling in at the beginning of a ride and *trusting the process* is more like when the roller coaster car starts its ascent. Can you hear the clicking on the track as it pulls you closer and closer to the top? Your heart races and your brain begins to question why you ever decided to get on this ride in the first place. You reach the top; the view is so beautiful; you gasp in excitement! You can see everything. You feel the wind blowing through your hair moments before the car drops, and then up and down you go through the loops and turns. Finally, you arrive safely back at the end of the ride. You survived! It was actually fun, and now you are no longer fearful, but excited to go back and do it all again. Each time you go, there is less fear and more excitement. Many of you are willing to *trust the process* with a safe (or not-so-safe) amusement ride, but are you ready to trust God with *wherever* He is leading you?

Sorbe

Yes! I can hear that familiar clicking sound in my mind, Johnson! It is a sound that I can easily recall and my heart beats just a little faster. My dad loved going on amusement rides with me and I never wanted to let him down. I would be brave for him. However, the first ascent was always the scariest part for me! My dad would attempt to distract me by saying, "Oh look! You can see the whole park from here. Isn't that great?!" *Gulp! I CAN see the whole park from here! Gahhh!* I learned how to labor-breathe before I even knew what that meant.

Jesus save me! Click...click...click...click click click–SCREAM!!!!! Can you tell I had some issues with that part of the ride? But every time I got off one of those rides, I was ready to get back on. Okay, Johnson, please do go on. These people are ready for this ride!

Johnson

I'm excited, Sorbe! Before we dig further into this section, please take some time to consider and answer these questions. Do you have a hard time trusting? What things make it challenging for you to trust people or God? What situations from your past have kept you from stepping out in faith?

Daily walking, listening, and trusting God is not always easy. Sometimes things happen that may cause us to question what God is doing. I needed to learn to trust the process. At this point in my life, Sorbe and I were talking on the phone and praying regularly, usually in the morning before our kids were awake. Those intentional moments with Sorbe were a lifeline...it felt very much like talking to an emergency dispatcher. "Madam, how can I help you? What is your emergency?" My response, "Today an eagle hit my car! My husband is mentally gone, and I am not sure if his brain will ever recover...I miss him. A good-sized rock fell from an overpass and hit my car window! My oldest daughter was sledding at church, and she ended up breaking not her first but second bone this year." This active sharing and processing with Jenn helped me in so many ways. What began as me having a safe space to verbally vomit my pain turned into an intentional course of action. I cannot fully explain how amazing it felt to be able to do something. When you are living in a space where bad things are continually happening to you, it makes it hard to trust that God's plans are genuinely good.[1] Prayer was vital. Telling the Lord I was open to Him each day was revolutionary in my life. I started seeing Him show up daily in miraculous ways–over and over again. I still called Sorbe with the hard stuff, but the percentage of exciting God sightings began to slowly overtake the dramatic negative things. It was so nice to be able to breathe regularly and with ease again. And yet, though our God sightings were such an encouragement, my constant prayers for my husband to be healed seemed to be going unanswered.

Day after day my husband slept in a room in my grandmother's basement. Over a period of 2 years, my routine stayed much the same. I cared for and homeschooled my 6 children, and once they were tucked into bed (at my parents' house) I walked down a dimly lit sidewalk to see my husband. Sometimes he would be awake when I got there, but sometimes he was fast asleep. I prepared him a meal and we would sit in the dark, talking little to none, and watch mindless home improvement shows. My husband could no longer handle light or conversations–he could not even watch the football games he once loved. Mark, before his brain injury, had been such an extrovert. He got his energy from being around people. When we lived in southern Minnesota, he worked three jobs and never seemed to get tired. Even after long days at work he loved to invite people over. I so desperately missed the little things that I had taken for granted before. Many fall mornings after driving the school bus, he would stop by to bring me a pumpkin spice cappuccino before he headed off to church. He took care of the finances. He made all the paperwork calls that I hated...you know the ones where you are on hold for an eternity, and you may or may not accomplish anything. Mark and I would take turns driving our kids to different activities. All the things that had been so normal before felt like a distant, fading memory. I missed him.

Hopefully, you can sense the power in those times of prayer with Sorbe. God had sent her into my life so that I did not have to fight this battle alone. It helped me feel seen and not forsaken. At this time the high moments were pretty high, and the lows were pretty low. This lesson of *trusting the process* became very real for me at my lowest point. Sorbe and I were praying continually for my husband. We began praying that God would take him out of the darkness and into the light. Well, that prayer was answered but in a way that brought me to face my greatest fear...the possibility of losing him.

The kids and I had returned from a Saturday Night church service and were just getting out of the van when I got the call. It was Mark. There was urgency in his voice. "Something is wrong with my leg. I need you to come over–now."

I quickly handed the kids off to my parents and ran over to my husband. As I entered his room, I could see his engorged leg from the doorway. He was sitting in his chair; his leg was double its normal size and was blue. Mark had just had hernia surgery the week before; and, when I called my mom (a registered nurse) she said, "He likely has blood clots; he needs to get to the hospital right away."

Mark could not walk up the stairs, so we called an ambulance. The paramedics struggled to get my 6'9" husband out of the basement, but they eventually succeeded. Arriving at the hospital, Mark was quickly assessed and rushed back for scans and x-rays. The results immediately shot an image into my mind of me sitting with my 6 children in front of a casket. Moments like these are so clear. I can remember where I was standing, the cold tiled floor beneath my feet, looking back and forth between the doctor and my husband, who was being wheeled to another room. The doctor's eyes and tone whispered, *I am so sorry, Mrs. Johnson.*

"Can I talk to you privately for a moment? It is a good thing you called the ambulance when you did...your husband has a massive clot that runs from his ankle all the way up into his abdomen. At any time, if even a piece of it breaks off, he will die. It is even possible that it could have been released if he had walked up the stairs, and he wouldn't be here right now. We need to surgically remove the clot...every second we wait, puts him at risk of it releasing and killing your husband. Oh, and Mrs. Johnson, there is one more thing. When we did the scan on your husband, we discovered a large mass on his liver. Whenever we see clots paired with a mass, cancer is a likely possibility. So, if he lives through this we will check into the cancer. But please don't tell your husband yet. He has enough to think about right now."

Shock, a heavy weight of fear and responsibility, washed over me. My Dad was standing in the hallway waiting for me to explain what was going on. I told him everything. I cried, he hugged me, and he simply said, "Jenny, I am so sorry."

He left to make phone calls to our family so I could focus on Mark and not have to repeat the doctor's words over and over. While Mark was preparing for surgery, I called my brother, Dan, for support. I want you to know that I never swear....ever. But at that moment, I used the worst word in my vocabulary; I cried, "Dan, this situation is so...so....so...crappy! I am so tired of this."

My brother said, "Jenny, crappy is what I say when someone accidentally puts mayonnaise on my sandwich. This situation is @#$%#@!" I normally would not have appreciated my brother's swearing, but in that instance, I felt so loved by his empathy and anger over my situation.

After talking to my brother, I called Sorbe and repeated his words to her. She laughed through tears. "Jenny, God is so good! He knows how hard this situation is and he is sending people to swear on your behalf. That thing that you cannot do in your own power, the Lord is doing for you."

I can't tell you how true those words felt, right then.

Sorbe

How do you respond, when your friend who has been facing all sorts of terrible hardship, calls you with this information? You cry with her. We had been praying to the Lord to get Mark out of that basement. Little did we know that this is how our prayer would be answered. However, I remained hope-filled that God had a plan while Johnson was in the thick of it. After that call, I stepped into a new place of prayer. I just couldn't accept a death sentence over Mark. I would have to take up the shield of faith[2] that Johnson so desperately needed at this time. I prayed, "God you did not answer our prayer to get Mark out of that dark, lonely basement only to take him from us." With that shield, I stood in prayer and began to intercede for his life.

Johnson

I just want to say thank you to Jenn Sorbe for her faithful prayers! Seriously, those of you who have faced long difficult seasons may understand, I was too tired to pray anything more than simple robotic prayers. I was in a very real battle, I needed God to send reinforcements. The Lord sent so many people to pray, offer help, and give words of encouragement for me and my family. Prayer really did make all the difference. My husband did not die in the basement with all those clots!

The surgery went well; but his time in the hospital revealed an unexpected discovery–a bleed in his neck called a dissection. This bleed had likely been there from the car accident, restricting some blood flow to his brain. If Mark had not gone to the hospital for the clots, this bleed would likely have never been discovered. This was good, but I could not stop thinking about the cancer. My children had watched in horror from my parent's window, as their father was carried out on a stretcher. They had all been praying for their dad to get better and this was far from what they had been asking of God. One of my children even voiced, "Mom, we keep praying for Daddy to get better, but he keeps getting worse."

My daughter's words weighed heavy on my heart as I drove my husband to get answers concerning the cancer. They took Mark back and while I was in the waiting room I began to desperately negotiate with God, "Lord, how about not cancer? How about fatty liver disease? Or you know...he is on a lot of medications–maybe they have really damaged his liver."

This was God's response: "Jenny, why do you always assume I am going to give you something bad?" I don't think I have ever reacted to God before in this way, but I felt exasperated, "God, do you not see what I am going through? Look at my life!" No response....but I could not stop thinking over His words, *"Why do you always assume I am going to give you something bad?"*

So, what was it? Was it cancer? Was it a fatty liver? Or an organ messed up by too many medications? No. It was a scar. Another missed injury from the car accident. In the crash Mark's seat belt had caused a lacerated liver and internal bleeding! He could have died from this hidden wound, but the liver had "healed itself." What we thought was cancer was actually God revealing a miracle. This is what I told my children: "Do you remember all those times we prayed for Daddy to get better? Well, God was healing him in a way we couldn't see. He had internal bleeding, but it was healed."[3]

"WHY DO YOU ALWAYS ASSUME I AM GOING TO GIVE YOU SOMETHING BAD?"

That was how I learned to trust the process. It was with His words, "Why do you always assume I am going to give you something bad?" What looked like a slap in the face from God was Him answering the very thing I had requested of Him. He brought my husband out of that basement. The clots that *should have* killed him, didn't. On the contrary, they led to the discovery of something that was limiting blood flow to his brain! The "possible cancer" turned into a hidden miracle. WOW! God works in ways that we could never expect or even imagine. That was, in a sense, my first roller coaster ride...or at least the light bulb moment for me. Getting on the ride was inviting God into my situation; *trust the process* was learning that even when things looked nothing like how I thought they should, God was still good and trustworthy.

Sorbe

When something bad happens, you have three choices:

1. Let it define you
2. Let it destroy you
3. Let it strengthen you

> *"Now a certain man was sick, Lazarus of Bethany, the village of Mary and her sister Martha. It was Mary who anointed the Lord with ointment, and wiped His feet with her hair, whose brother Lazarus was sick. So the sisters sent word to Him, saying, 'Lord, behold, he whom You love is sick.'"*
>
> John 11:1-3 (NASB)

Jesus states Lazarus will not die. We know he does, in fact, die and is subsequently placed in a tomb. Lazarus is dead for four days before Jesus even shows up! What did Jesus mean by saying Lazarus would not die? He hears the urgent news of a person who needs him and whom he loves, but he STAYS where He's at for two more days, on purpose, after hearing the news so Lazarus could die! Wow.

But we know Christ's Character...

- *He loves these three because he loves people.*

- *He has a plan.*
- *He has not forgotten them.*
- *He has not ignored them (though they likely think He has).*
- *He takes His time acting on their behalf.*
- *He has a reason for His timing, and it is always an opportunity for us to level up (grow/deepen) in our faith.*

They obviously want healing done in their timing. We're learning Jesus doesn't always step in to answer our requests when we think He should. He sees a larger picture we cannot see. (For those of you who like looking things up, check out God's response to Habakkuk in Habakkuk 1:5. I often paraphrase it to, "If you could see what I (God) am doing behind the scenes, it would blow your mind.") Regardless, God is smarter and sees more than we do. Let's continue our story!

So, when the time is right, He tells the disciples that Lazarus "has fallen asleep." He's only ready to go back once He knows Lazarus is dead. In verse 15, He says, "Lazarus is dead, and for your sake I am glad I was not there, so that you may believe. But let's go to him." Important note: If we don't know Jesus's character–who He is–we will be so offended by the above statement, "I'm glad I was not there..." *Wait...what? I thought you loved me! You healed people you didn't even know! They weren't even doing ministry for you, and you healed them on the spot! But me? The one you love, the one you know. You... WAIT! You're even glad about it?!* Stunned. Offended. Hurt. Losing faith.

BUT...AND OFTEN WITH JESUS, THERE IS A BUT.

But...and often with Jesus, there is a but. BUT if we know Jesus for who He is, we will not be deceived by these thoughts. We will be patient. We will see the story through to the miraculous end. We will *trust the process*.

WE WILL SEE THE STORY THROUGH TO THE MIRACULOUS END. WE WILL *TRUST THE PROCESS.*

Another interesting turn of events comes in the second half of John, chapter 11, starting in verse 21. Enter Martha onto the scene. She comes out to greet Jesus and relays a very powerful statement, "If you had been here my brother would not have died. But I know even now God will give you whatever you ask..." Wow, Go Martha! Martha gets such a bad rep when stories are told about her. In Luke 10:38-42, she is trying to be a good host to Jesus and His disciples, but her attitude and perspective in that moment were off and so Jesus called her out on it. Mary gets the compliment that day because she longed to sit at the feet of Jesus. She received the greater blessing, and we give ourselves permission to talk bad about Martha. Personally, that's never set well with me; Martha was trying her best that day. But God gave her a powerful truth through His interaction with her.

> *Martha*: "Lord, do you not care that my sister has left me to serve alone? Tell her then to help me."
>
> *Jesus*: "Martha, Martha, you are anxious and troubled about many things, but one thing is necessary. Mary has chosen the good portion, which will not be taken away from her."

HE WAS GIVING HER PERMISSION TO REST IN HIM.

Martha wasn't doing anything wrong, but her priorities were off. It's okay that they were because she learned that day what they should be. She was trying to be a good hostess for which a guest could give his gratitude, but Jesus knew she would receive a much greater blessing if she would just sit at his feet. He was giving her permission to REST in Him. How many of us need to learn to rest? We work hard for our families and at our jobs, but do we take the time necessary to rest at the feet of Jesus? I'm so thankful we were able to see this all play out in front of us. We may get offended when someone tells us to just sit down and relax, but we should see it as a blessing. Rest is so very important that even God, himself, did it.[4]

Johnson

My turn to interrupt! I love this so much. Sorbe knows her Bible. I have totally judged Martha and will never see her the same way again. She truly was a woman of faith and blunt, honest truth. I am on the edge of my seat, excited to learn. Preach it sister!

Sorbe

Alright, Martha was speaking a powerful truth to Jesus in the midst of terrible suffering. "But I know even now God will give you whatever you ask..." Now, on to Mary. Verse 20 says the following, "So when Martha heard that Jesus was coming, she went and met him, but Mary remained seated in the house." Mary didn't go greet Jesus, she stayed...seated. Lazarus is dead. People have come from a nearby town to comfort and mourn with the sisters. She is sad and mourning her loss. Jesus didn't arrive, like she hoped he would, to save her brother from death. This is how I see the moment playing out, "I told Jesus Lazarus was sick and he didn't come! I sat at His feet. I listened to Him. But He didn't come when I needed him most. He could've saved my brother, but He chose to stay away. You go ahead and meet him Martha, but I'm not going to. He's hurt me too much. I'm staying here to feel sorry for myself and just grieve and be mad." Now, obviously this is conjecture on my part, but it's how I see that moment when I read that Mary remained seated. I've been hurt by people and my first inclination when they show up on my doorstep is certainly not to run into their arms. But Jesus is no ordinary person, He is the son of God, and both the sisters are just beginning to come to this realization. Maybe they don't fully see the big picture, yet. But they are about to.

HE MAKES CLEAR OUR NEED TO *KNOW* HIM SO THAT WE DON'T LOSE OUR HOPE IN MOMENTS OF DESPAIR. IF WE RESOLVE TO TRUST HIM FULLY, HE WILL RESURRECT OUR SLEEPING FAITH.

Jesus answers Martha, in verse 23, in an interesting way, telling her that her brother will rise again. She thinks He's speaking of the resurrection of the dead on the last day. I don't know why Jesus sometimes answers people this way. I wish He wouldn't do this, but He does. This is how he works. It's not rude. He makes us really step out in our faith. He allows us to be a part of the process. He pushes us like a parent pushing her child on their little bike without training wheels. He makes clear our need to *know* Him so that we don't lose our hope in moments of despair. If we resolve to trust Him fully, He will resurrect our sleeping faith.

They continue their conversation in verses 25 and 26. "Jesus said to her, 'I am the resurrection and the life. Whoever believes in me, though he dies, yet shall he live, and everyone who lives and believes in me shall never die. Do you believe this?' Martha responds to him, 'Yes, Lord; I believe that you are the Christ, the Son of God, who is coming into the world.'" He then tests her (our) faith with His next question by allowing Martha to come along with him. He is ultimately leading her mind into full understanding. He asks, "Do you believe?" (And if *we* say yes and mean it, we are about to receive the miracle!)

Ok, now Mary comes. Jesus has asked for her. She loves Jesus, so this excites her heart to hear that He's specifically requesting her presence. However, she is going to let Him know how He let her down when she sees Him. In verse 32, Mary drops to her face in front of Jesus, sobbing. Once again, I will give you what I hear in my thoughts as I read this part. "Jesus! If you had been here, I wouldn't be grieving my brother! I wouldn't have to be feeling this pain and anguish. You could've prevented my suffering! Where were you? Why didn't you come when I called...in my timing?!" Jesus is moved by her emotions, her tormented sadness. The Bible says he was "deeply moved and troubled," and He asks them to show him where Lazarus is laid. When they reply, "come and see Lord," He weeps.

Why? Why is he moved in His spirit and troubled by this emotional outpouring by Mary? Why did he weep when they replied, "come and see, Lord [where we put his dead body]?" When he gets to the tomb, Jesus is yet again deeply moved. He asks them to roll away the stone–to open the tomb. Now Martha, who just moments ago told Jesus, "I know even now God will give you whatever you ask," is saying something entirely different. Has her faith gone? She worriedly replies, "But Jesus, he's been dead for four days. He's going to be stinky." Martha had so much faith, and then–poof–back to earthly thoughts. What changed?

Jesus responds with a reminder of his previous declaration. By the way, I really love how Jesus responds in moments like these. People are sobbing; questioning his plan–even though they've seen him do miracles before. He doesn't get mad. He just speaks the truth with a calm authority that calls all in attendance to wait with bated breath. This moment will be like nothing they had ever dreamed or expected. Dead is dead. *Right?*

Jesus is plainly, without sarcasm, stating a truth–and a powerful one at that. "Did I not tell you that if you believe you will see the glory of God?

"Then move the stone."

Imagine you are standing there, too. You are beginning to realize that this man, Jesus, whom you have really come to love and adore, is planning to do something really crazy. *But what if it doesn't work?* Faith and fear collide. The men move the stone aside. Those near the tomb obey Jesus' *seemingly stupid* request. And then–and I love this–Jesus goes to the Father, in prayer, on our behalf. Wow.

"Father, I thank you that you have heard me. I know that you always hear me, but I said this for the benefit of the people standing here, that they may believe that you sent me."

How awesome that he does this for us? How awesome that he speaks words in a way in which we can get the real, and true, powerful message! We can be so full of our own thoughts, back and forth in our emotions and needing to be led through to greener pastures. Our loving Shepherd... The One who protects us from the wolves trying to devour us; unto the point of death. And He actually selflessly chooses to step in on our behalf. *He wants this job? Seriously?*

I believe. I don't believe. I believe. I don't believe. Jesus, you want this (pointing to myself, incredulously)? Yep. He knows. But he does it anyway. Anybody else floored by that kind of love? You should be. I am.

Okay, back to our story. Jesus says, in a loud voice, "Lazarus, come out!" And the guy who was dead for four long, tormenting days strolls out. Here's where we pass out and then rejoice and cry. A total mic drop moment for Jesus here. But Jesus just plainly states, "Take off the grave clothes and let him go." He's so chill. Because, He knows who he is. He knows his purpose. He knows where his power comes from. He knows and trusts the character of his father. And he lives it, speaks it, and obeys it. *Trust the Process.*

Group Discussion Questions/Action Step/ Personal Reflection/Journal:

Trust: Confidence; a reliance or resting of the mind on the integrity, veracity, justice, friendship, or other sound principle of another person.[5]

But whoever trusts in the Lord shall be safe.
Proverbs 29:25 (ESV)

- Examine the definition of trust provided above. What observations come to mind?

- Sorbe mentioned the word "rest" concerning Martha's busyness. What does rest look like for you? What do you think Jesus meant when he says we are to enter into His rest? (See Hebrews 4 & Psalm 95 for further study.)

- "He knows His purpose. He knows where His power comes from. He knows and trusts the character of His Father. And he lives it, speaks it, and obeys it." Using Sorbe's insights, can you name specific ways you are living, speaking, and obeying God?

Assignment: Trust the process...Write down something you are waiting for...maybe it is healing for a loved one who is sick, a broken family relationship restored, or an important decision to be made...it can be anything. Start praying about it with a friend. Keep praying and declaring until you see/experience breakthrough!

Prayer:

Dear Jesus,

I ask Your forgiveness for my unbelief when I didn't trust You. Speak to me Holy Spirit, Your truth about my situation and reveal to me how I can trust the process. I want to grow the faith You have already given me. I want to trust You, Lord, and Your timing. I want You in the driver's seat. I submit my will to You. Thank you for Your forgiveness, Your patience, and Your love for me. I love you too.

In Jesus' name I pray. Amen

7–SUCK IT UP AND DRIVE ON

"Obedience to God's will is the secret of spiritual knowledge and insight. It is not willingness to know, but willingness to DO (obey) God's will that brings certainty."
Eric Liddell

"Do you not know that if you present yourselves to anyone as obedient slaves, you are slaves of the one whom you obey, either of sin, which leads to death, or of obedience, which leads to righteousness?"
Romans 6:16 (ESV)

Sorbe

Earlier Johnson talked about the poor soul who chose to eat a beetle. No one in their right mind *wants* to do that, but isn't it interesting what we are willing to do sometimes? Peer-pressure has been around since nearly the beginning of time. Technology just makes it a lot easier to keep the peer pressure going 24 hours a day. And it doesn't stop just because we grow up. Ever heard of the phrase, "keeping up with the Joneses?" We are often comparing ourselves to others or allowing others to maneuver our minds. I knew a young lady in middle school who was further developed than most of the girls her age. Boys began telling her that it was her obligation to send them photos of her "development." The sad fact was that she felt obligated to do so. Why? I wondered that...and she and I had some good chats back then; but ultimately, it was due to the fact she was unaware of where her true identity resided. She didn't realize her value. This girl had no clue she was created in the image and likeness of God with purpose, on purpose, and for a purpose. She didn't have the courage or the strength or the knowledge to stand up for herself and say, "No way do you deserve that from me!" Instead, her identity was resting in the views and expectations of other people; and those views swayed her. My heart broke for her and the many others who believed the lies the world was telling them instead of knowing who they were in Christ. I, too, believed these lies as I was growing up. Though my mom was speaking [God's] truth into my life, the pull of the world and the desire to be accepted by it was strong. As we talked about earlier, once saved in Christ, we have been given the mind of Christ; however, that doesn't mean we understand how to use it. Many of us have been swayed by someone else into doing something we did not want to do. We allowed people to influence us.[1] Though that is not always bad, it is important to know who is influencing our influencers. Is it Jesus or the devil? Allow me to share a couple of life stories with you.

Army Boot Camp gave me confidence. It was where I started to realize what I was capable of. Boot camp was about facing both personal and team challenges. I accepted and did the things I was told to do–even things that otherwise I might never have considered doing. It challenged me to be the best version of myself. I learned very quickly that giving up was not an option. Regardless of the challenge in front of us, we were taught to persevere. No matter what. Saying, *"I can't do it,"* was not tolerated. You get up and do what you're told to do. If something didn't go right, you find a solution to the problem and you don't quit until you do. No complaints either. You suck it up and drive on.

"IF YOU HAVE TO DO SOMETHING, YOU HAVE THREE CHOICES: YOU CAN DO IT AND LIKE IT, YOU CAN DO IT AND HATE IT, OR YOU CAN JUST DO IT."

For some, the challenges were too difficult a task and they wanted out. I found that I embraced them. My dad had a saying, "If you have to do something, you have three choices: You can do it and like it, you can do it and hate it, or you can just do it." He would go on with, "I choose to do it and like it. When you have to do it anyway, doing it with a happy attitude helps you get it done quickly and you move on. When you hate it, it makes it harder and the anger lingers, usually ruining your day." His words have stayed with me and given me an optimism towards challenges or duties in life that I've needed to do, even when I haven't wanted to do them. They've inspired me to keep going and not give up, believing that there are blessings on the other side of it all if I change my perspective. A big "Thanks!" to boot camp for sending that message home as well! Girls who joined and hated it either quit or they had a real hard time making it through to the end. They had bad attitudes about it all and well, it sucked to be them. I didn't want any part of that unhappy life. I told my brain, *'I am here. I chose to be here on my own accord. So, I may as well make the best of it.'* Little did I know that I was living out "Trust the Process".

Boot camp is about training you to become a soldier. More importantly, more specifically, it is learning how to obey orders without question. Before they could instill that in you, they needed to break your pride, your spirit, and your individuality. You were not the *one*. You were a *team* and, like it or not, you would learn to work together. You were assigned a battle buddy and it was pounded into your head that 'you never leave your battle buddy behind.' Whatever task was assigned to you, you did it–no questions asked. You don't like what they're asking you to do? Well, suck it up and drive on, soldier! You've got a job to do, and you no longer own yourself. The government owns you. You signed the papers. You are the Army's solution to the government's problems, and they are going to see to it that you are highly trained and very obedient.

Many of you probably know or have heard that in boot camp they push your physical and mental limits daily. I heard it said that, "We do more by 10 a.m. than most people do all day." Our superiors pushed us further than we knew we could go physically. Once they pushed our physical bodies to their known limits, our minds needed to step in to keep us going. Most people stop when their bodies get tired. Athletes, or in this scenario soldiers, are taught to push past their tired muscles and go beyond their bodies' natural limits. This, you see, is a part of the process. As the drill sergeants continued to exercise us, muscle failure would begin to set into our arms and legs. Muscle failure is where your body begins to shake and can no longer do the exercise. The Army is intentional in doing this during training because they are building more than just our muscles–they are also strengthening our minds. Ever heard of "mind over matter"? This is your brain's ability to use its will over your body. I would yell in my mind, "Go! Don't stop! Just another one...another one...another one! Don't you quit on me, body! I'm the boss, not you!" When you are pushed past your limits...you're shaking, sweating, desperate; and then, rest–if only for a moment. "FALL IN!" the drill sergeant yells, and immediately we jump up to form our organized lines and march back to our barracks to shower quickly. Breakfast would be our reward and then on to the next task.

My father told me a story recently about his time serving in the Vietnam War. He has been reading our book as we write it and our stories have reminded him of some of his own. Some I have heard, but others I have not. He learned some hard lessons over there and believes God kept him alive. I had the great honor of serving in the same aviation unit as my dad when I first joined. He was well loved by many people. His reputation of being a very skilled helicopter pilot, along with his humor and confidence, followed his name. So naturally, everywhere I would go in military circles, it was inevitable that someone would recognize that same last name sewn onto my uniform, and they were sure to share stories with me. Let me share one of his memories with you.

Knowing the draft is coming for him, my father proactively goes into the recruiting station to sign up. He wants to pick his job in the military rather than have the government decide. He wants to be a pilot. At 18 years old, he heads off to Fort Polk for boot camp and then to flight school where he is certified to fly UH-1 Huey, Hughes TH-55 Osage, and Bell OH-13 Helicopters. One year after joining the Army, he is shipped off to war.

The year is 1968. My dad is now 20 years old and is the chief pilot on a resupply mission along with three other guys: a co-pilot, a crew chief, and a gunner. They are heading from Kon Tum, Vietnam, north of Pleiku, to resupply a fire base unit in the jungle, and their chopper is loaded with ammunition. They have already done three or four missions like this today. Though there is always a risk on these missions, no intel has come in to deter their route. Five minutes into this flight, they know they won't make it to their destination.

Their aircraft is shot by enemy ground fire with a 50-caliber bullet. It hits the push-pull tube, which controls the main blade. This causes one of the two main rotor blades, which are tilted, to go flat, no longer pitching it correctly. The aircraft's nose drops straight down. Immediately, my father manhandles the collective together with the cyclic and slams his feet with all his might against the anti-torque pedals, but nothing happens. He has lost complete control of the entire aircraft and puts out a mayday call. He hears someone yelling "Jesus" and "Momma." (Later in the day, they all admit they heard those cries, but no one knows who was the one who yelled it.)

The chopper flips a 180. As a consequence, the tail slams into the ground, which likely saves the men's lives. The aircraft's nose slams forward into the thick jungle. In the process, with him still strapped to it, my father's chair hurls him through the windshield and into the canopy of trees. His hands instinctively fly up to protect his face. His chair gets tangled up in the jumbled branches and hangs upside down about 6 feet above the ground.

The downed aircraft, filled with its ammo load, is now engulfed in flames. Adrenalin now coursing through his body, dazed and confused by the impact, my father attempts to regain his bearings. He sees what appears to be a Viet Cong running on the sky toward him. The ceramic chicken plate he wears to protect his chest from bullets is pushing on his throat, cutting off his air supply. A bullet hits him in the chest, and he hears machine gun fire. The Viet Cong soldier that he saw running on the sky, drops dead. One of the crew cuts my dad loose. He falls hard from the trees to the ground, only now realizing that he has been upside down. Back to his senses, he knows they are going to be swarmed by the enemy in minutes. He and his crew begin to run. Bullets are flying everywhere. They enter a clearing to find an awaiting Army chopper. By God's grace, they make it to the safety of their own encampment, alive.

Back at the field hospital, x-rays are taken, and the men sit outside drinking coffee awaiting their results. Two doctors step out to report their findings. The co-pilot, holding his coffee, is told he has a broken collarbone. Immediately, he drops his cup and passes out. Next, the crew chief is told he has a broken leg. Immediately, he faints and his body sags out of the chair to the floor. Bewildered by what he's witnessing, my dad wonders what will happen when the doctor comes to me? (Mind you, they all ran out of the crash area without knowing they had any injuries, using all their limbs just fine.)

The doctor, now facing my father, "Chief, you have two broken wrists and fractured ribs from the bullet hitting the chicken plate." Instantly, my dad goes unconscious and slides to the floor. The gunner, readying himself to be the next to pass out, is informed that he has some minor bruising but otherwise is in good shape. With a relieved chuckle, he resigns to lean back against the wall to finish his cup of coffee and his smoke. The gunner later relays the scene to the crew when they regain consciousness. Interestingly, my father also says that as they all sat waiting for the doctors to come out, they thought they were talking to one another. The nurses informed them however, they were, in fact, stone silent.

Johnson

Wow! The drive to push past our physical limits is truly incredible. Not giving up, pushing through, is such a desirable trait. I want that! Love this story of real heroism. Absolutely, inspiring!

Sorbe

I'm with you Johnson! Those soldiers' bodies responded in ways that were necessary in order to survive. Both consciously and unconsciously they pushed beyond their own natural limits because they had no other choice. My father had not recognized any pain while hanging upside down in the wrecked aircraft, or even when he was shot in the chest, breaking his ribs. Both his wrists had been broken when he slammed through the windshield, yet he was able to use his weapon to counter fire as they ran to the awaiting chopper. The soldiers' minds protected them to keep them alive; it wasn't until the doctor relayed the extent of their injuries that they finally were able to feel.

†

THE MORE PASSIONATE WE FELT, THE MORE POWERFUL AND INDOMITABLE WE BECAME.

In the early morning physical training sessions at boot camp, our drill sergeants would ask us if we wanted more PT. Already spent and tired it seemed like a cruel joke, but we would yell back, "Yes Drill Sergeant! Make it hurt, Drill Sergeant, make it hurt!" In these moments I noticed a strengthening in my spirit. An indomitable spirit, if you will. This is the same kind of spirit I believe kept my dad alive. You see, the point was not the pain. It was how to move through the pain towards growth. Our teachers had already learned what we were learning. And though our limbs would be shaking and our bodies spent, we were beginning to realize our minds could make our bodies do what was necessary to persevere. We no longer asked to quit. We no longer laid down. We faced whatever was in front of us head on, and the more passionate we felt, the more powerful and indomitable we became.

We were getting stronger, both mentally and physically, becoming more resilient and meshing as a team. If ever our bodies failed us, we had our battle buddies next to us, picking us up and keeping us moving. Quitting was not an option. Obedience was always expected. *Obey, don't think, just do. Trust. Do. Never quit*. This was a very important lesson in my life.

Side note: As I was writing this portion of the book, this song came on in the background and it gave me pause. I feel that I should share it with you.

"Fix My Eyes"
by for KING & COUNTRY

"...Here's what I'd do differently.
I'd love like I'm not scared. Give when it's not fair. Live life for another. Take time for a brother. Fight for the weak ones. Speak out for freedom. Find faith in the battle. Stand tall but above it all. Fix my eyes on you, on you...
I learned the lines and talked the talk

(Everybody knows that, everybody knows that).
But the road less traveled is hard to walk
(Everybody knows that, everybody knows).
It takes a soldier, who knows his orders,
To walk the walk I'm supposed to walk."[2]

I didn't know it then, but my military experience would strengthen my prayer life. One of my favorite verses I memorized in my teen years was, "For though we walk in the flesh, we do not war after the flesh: For the weapons of our warfare are not carnal, but mighty through God to the pulling down of strong holds" (2 Corinthians 10:3-4). In the Army, you are trained to wage war against the "flesh," aka humans. Our war is not against people. So, what is it against? It is against the devil and his demons that were thrown out of heaven.

> *Your hand-to-hand combat is not with human beings, but with the highest principalities and authorities operating in rebellion under the heavenly realms. For they are a powerful class of demon-gods and evil spirits that hold this dark world in bondage. Because of this, you must wear all the armor that God provides so you're protected as you confront the slanderer, for you are destined for all things and will rise victorious.*
>
> Ephesians 6:12-13 (TPT)

Let me just mention, quickly, that God has *already given us* our weapons for this warfare. By battling using God's weapons (Eph 6:17, Heb 4:12), wearing our heavenly armor (Eph 6:14-18), tapping into our Christ-like mind (1 Cor 2:16), and rejoice and praying continually (1 Thes 5:16-18), we can and will pull down the strongholds of the enemy. Do you know what? You and me, we are all soldiers, and this life is our boot camp. So, we need to know our orders to walk the walk we're supposed to walk. And not just to survive, but to thrive and live victoriously. How? By putting God in control of it all. Step in, soldier. This is your battle call.

Johnson

TRUSTING THE LORD REQUIRES PRACTICE.

"Quitting was not an option. Obedience was always the choice. *Obey, don't think, just do. Trust. Do. Never quit.*" I love this quote from Sorbe on *trust the process*! Trusting the Lord requires practice. As you begin actively listening and obeying, the Lord will develop beautiful heroic qualities in you. Persevering through hard things produces character.[3] This brings to mind someone who did not trust the process but did understand God's character... Jonah. Please feel free to dig deeper and read the book of Jonah. It is only four short chapters. He is our next example of stupid.

Jonah was a prophet. This means it was his job to receive messages from the Lord and deliver them in God's timing. Jonah would have understood what it meant to be appointed by God as a prophet. He would have understood both the privilege and risk involved in this sometimes-dangerous calling. Often, prophets were asked to bring harsh messages to dangerous people. Firefighters are called to run into burning buildings. Navy Seals are called to rescue hostages. ER nurses, underwater welders, search and rescue teams... They all understand the risks involved in their respective occupations. What would you think of a firefighter who based saving a man on how worthy he felt that man was of being saved? This line of thinking brings us to our story.

> *"The word of the Lord came to Jonah, son of Amittai: 'Go to the great city of Nineveh and preach against it, because its wickedness has come up before me.' But Jonah ran away from the Lord and headed for Tarshish. He went down to Joppa, where he found a ship bound for that port. After paying the fare, he went aboard and sailed for Tarshish to flee from the Lord."*
>
> Jonah 1:1-3 (NIV)

This is the biggest assignment of Jonah's life...and he runs. His motivation for fleeing comes directly from his negative feelings towards God's desire to give the people of Nineveh an opportunity to change. Jonah does not feel these people are worthy of rescuing, so he avoids the assignment by disobeying God and running. This seems foolish to me. He knew God had the ability to destroy Nineveh for their disobedience. This is what I want to say to Jonah...

> *"You are supposed to be a Prophet. You were called to deliver a message telling people they must obey or else bad things will happen to them and you respond by disobeying God? You must know that you are being quite the hypocrite. You are acting just like the people you hate; except, in this case, your disobedience is worse!"*

At the very end of the book, God reveals why Jonah's disobedience is worse. Let's read Jonah 4:11. "But the Lord said to Jonah, 'And should I not have concern for the great city of Nineveh, in which there are more than a hundred and twenty thousand people who cannot tell their right hand from their left—and also many animals?'"

Here it says that the people of Nineveh did not know they were doing wrong things; whereas Jonah *did* know he was disobeying, and he chose to do so anyway. His behavior is worse and, may I say, more stupid. James 4:17 states, "So whoever knows the right thing to do and fails to do it, for him it is sin" (ESV). This is like deliberately choosing to place your hand on a hot stove knowing you will get burned. In response to Jonah's willful disobedience, God could have easily sank the boat he was on, let Jonah drown, and use his death as an example to future prophets. But God is not only patient and gracious with Nineveh, but He also has this very same grace for Jonah. Jonah is an avoider, but I have to give him some credit: if he is asked a question and can't run, he is incredibly honest. Jonah knows God well enough to know that the storm erupting in the sea he is in is the result of his direct disobedience to God's orders. In other words, the storm they're experiencing is his fault. Jonah tells the sailors they must throw him in the sea if they want the storm to stop. Reluctantly, the men do what Jonah commands and the tumultuous waters still. The sailors' response to witnessing this miracle resulted in a sincere fear and reverence of the Lord.

Jonah sinks and is close to drowning, but God sends a fish to swallow him, thus saving his life. It is in this dark space Jonah prays. He thanks the Lord for coming to his aid, but he doesn't apologize or say he will make things right by going to Nineveh. Rather, he says in Jonah 2:8-9, "Those who cling to worthless idols turn away from God's love for them. But I, with shouts of grateful praise, will sacrifice to you. What I have vowed I will make good. I will say, 'Salvation comes from the Lord.'" He definitely acknowledges God saving him, but even in his not very real-seeming apology, he puts himself above Nineveh; he basically says, "Idol worshipers turn away from you, but not me, God."

After his prayer, the fish spits Jonah out onto dry land. God doesn't bring up Jonah's prayer, he simply tells him to go to Nineveh and deliver the message. Jonah is being obedient at this point, but it reminds me of what Sorbe's father told her. "If you have to do something, you have three choices. You can do it and like it, you can do it and hate it, or you can just do it." Jonah chose to do it and hate it. This kind of heart leads us to the end of the story. Jonah has already delivered the message and is sitting on a hill, watching and hoping the people will not repent. He is longing for Nineveh to reject God and receive what they deserve–judgment.

And now for the "happy ending" moment of the story–the people repent! Salvation has come for them, just like it had for Jonah! But Jonah, instead of rejoicing, decides to ruin this perfect "Disney ending" for me. He is not just unhappy, he is angry. He is so furious that he screams the full truth of what is in his heart. Jonah 4:2-3 says, "Isn't this what I said, Lord, when I was still at home? That is what I tried to forestall by fleeing to Tarshish. I knew that you are a gracious and compassionate God, slow to anger and abounding in love, a God who relents from sending calamity. Now, Lord, take away my life, for it is better for me to die than to live."

God replies, "Is it right for you to be angry?" This question may seem odd at first, but it is absolutely perfect. Does Jonah have the right to complain about God's compassion, grace, slowness to anger, abounding love, and his desire to not send calamity? No. This prophet is actually scolding the Creator of the universe for the very qualities that were responsible for saving his life. He has gone from vowing to proclaim God's goodness and salvation to condemning God's goodness and salvation.

Sorbe

Dude. Seriously. Loving this, Johnson!

Johnson

It is easy to look at Jonah and feel disgust. He was such a bitter, hypocritical, and vengeful person. But the more I position myself in a place of moral superiority over him, the more I realize this is the heart of Jonah. I may have grace for the people of Nineveh, but I have very little grace for this disobedient prophet. Who has grace for Jonah? God. Most scholars believe that Jonah himself is the author of his book. I love this. It means that Jonah obeyed God in writing an entire book that made him look bad. How many of God's chosen people who heard this story could personally identify with Jonah's response towards Nineveh? This is a powerful example of someone who really struggled to *trust the process*. Jonah knew God's character, but he did not fully *value* it. He believed his own plans for Nineveh were better. He didn't want to participate in God's will for his life. He eventually did what God asked but not with joy or excitement. Are you a Jonah? What thing or things has God asked you to do that you are not doing?

Sorbe

I feel the need to interject here. Not long ago I learned of the term *dissonance*. It is the inconsistency between the beliefs you or I hold. In other words, dissonance is the inconsistency between our actions versus what we say we believe. An example might be someone who says they want to live a long and healthy life (even though they smoke and eat fast food, knowing these things are unhealthy and destructive to their bodies). You see, just because we say it doesn't mean we believe it. We may say we do, but we live out what we really believe–like me in learning to be open to God. I thought I trusted God fully until that trust was put to the test. It was only then I realized my stated belief did not jive with how I was living my life. I feel like not coming to this realization was Jonah's problem.

Johnson

Jonah, when asked to go, was honest with his opposition to God's plan, but he still ran away. When God calls us to do something and we don't want to do it, stalling and seeking distractions are the passive road we take to run away. We make so many excuses, and many of these excuses and their resulting actions leave us with a story, like Jonah's, that we would be embarrassed reading. I don't want a Jonah life and you don't either. I want a worm life. Allow me to explain. Who was appointed by God in this story and obeyed? A fish, a plant, and a worm. The fish obeyed, and a man was saved. God appointed a plant to rise up to provide shade for Jonah while he sulked and hoped God would destroy Nineveh. But the worm is my favorite example of obeying God in this story! When it was *appointed by the Lord* to destroy the plant and bring about the conclusion to Jonah's pity party, this was its reaction.

> *"When dawn came the next day, God appointed a worm that attacked the plant so that it withered."*
>
> Jonah 4:7 9 (BSB)

> *"But God prepared a worm when the morning rose the next day, and it smote the gourd that it withered."*
>
> Jonah 4:7 (KJV)

I DO NOT WANT TO BE LESS OBEDIENT THAN A WORM.

I love this so incredibly much! Have you ever heard of a smiting, attacking worm! We know that God is ultimately the hero of this story, but if I were to choose an earthly hero the prize would most definitely go to the worm. It obeyed with much finesse and passionate determination. It did not run away when appointed by God for an important mission. It obeyed God the first time. I do not want to be less obedient than a worm. I want to do the things God asks me to do and actually love the assignment, trusting that His plans are better than mine. I don't want to obey out of obligation while stomping my feet the whole way. *Trusting the process* is knowing and seeking out what God wants you to do. God's plans are good, even if we don't initially like what He tells us. This is your moment to step in and *trust the process*. Maybe there is someone God has asked you to forgive. You have gifts that God has given you to use for His Glory–are you using them? Are there painful parts of your life that God is wanting to free you from? Where are you on your Jonah journey? You have been asked to do something and I can promise you this: God's plans are good. The road He is having you walk to accomplish these plans is also good. Time for you to take your first step toward your Nineveh.

Group Discussion Questions/Action Step/ Personal Reflection/Journal:

- How can you apply the soldier scenario that Sorbe talks about to your own life? How do you see yourself as a soldier for God?

- In what ways has God asked you to "don't think, just do," as Sorbe described in her boot camp experience?

- What areas do you see spiritual/biblical dissonance in your life? What verses do you believe but recognize that you are not living out in your life?

Assignment: Take a leap of faith. Step into something outside your comfort zone. (Examples: Go on a mission trip, pray out loud with/ for a friend who's just shared some hard stuff with you, share your testimony on a social platform, at church, with your family, deliver a meal to whomever God directs, write thank you cards to everyone God lays on your heart...possibilities are limitless... please have fun with this challenge!)

Prayer:

Dear Jesus, I want to love others like you did, without fear. I want to give when it's not fair and take time for a brother. I want to fight for the weak ones and speak out for freedom. I want to find faith in the battle and stand tall above it all. I fix my eyes on You, Lord! You will show me the way. You will tend to my needs. You will never let me down, my anchor, my hope, my shelter. Thank You Lord!

In Jesus' name I pray. Amen

8–PERMISSION TO ASK QUESTIONS

"And the people of Berea were more open-minded than those in Thessalonica, and they listened eagerly to Paul's message. They searched the Scriptures day after day to see if Paul and Silas were teaching the truth."
Acts 17:11 (NLT)

"Ask, and it will be given to you; seek, and you will find; knock, and it will be opened to you. For everyone who asks receives, and the one who seeks finds, and to the one who knocks it will be opened. Or which one of you, if his son asks him for bread, will give him a stone? Or if he asks for a fish, will give him a serpent? If you then, who are evil, know how to give good gifts to your children, how much more will your Father who is in heaven give good things to those who ask him!"
Matthew 7:7-11 (ESV)

Johnson

The day I quit enjoying math was the day I stopped asking questions. I am, by nature, a word person and a verbal processor. I am also a relational person. My younger elementary school years were lovely–less desk time, more kinesthetic learning, and reading books inside a huge cardboard tree. Math was done on paper and with blocks. My teachers seemed happy, often encouraging us to discover and ask questions. If I didn't understand something, I felt comfortable asking for help. This "help," given by a loving authority, was really the perfect environment for me to learn and to grow. I have one tender memory with an extra sweet teacher who, during a test, could have easily been annoyed by my question. Instead, she knelt by my chair and gently explained my assignment.

Junior High was a vastly different experience. Entering this new environment, I found teachers were tired of answering questions. Years of having to deal with disrespectful and, may I say, verbally abusive students had left them haggard. The job they had once loved had become an obligation. My questions were seen as a threat, perceived by my teachers as a poor reflection on their ability to teach. Kids who asked questions were made to feel stupid and were verbally accosted in front of the class. This was when I decided to become invisible. My entire time in math was spent praying the teacher would never ask me a question, because I knew I would not know the answer. I eventually fell so far behind in class that I no longer tried to understand Algebra. I felt I was just too stupid to "get it." I began to believe a secondary lie as well... only dumb people ask questions. Without permission to ask questions, my learning of math came grinding to an immediate halt.

Asking questions is a vital part of *trust the process*. In this chapter, we are going to encourage you to bring your questions to the Lord. Diligently seeking God concerning His Word, your life and your circumstances cultivates a healthy environment for growth, life, and wisdom. Acts 17:11 will set the tone for this chapter. Paul and Silas presented the Gospel to the Bereans, and they did not immediately accept it. They listened to what the men had to say and checked to see if it lined up with the Old Testament Scripture. As they sought answers through faithfully seeking God, their questions were answered.

GOD IS BIG ENOUGH TO HANDLE ANY QUESTION YOU MAY HAVE FOR HIM. THIS IS YOUR PERMISSION TO QUESTION.

The NLT calls the Bereans open-minded, but other translations call them noble. My prayer for all of us is that we would be noble in our questioning, and we would long for understanding and wisdom. The fear of questions stunts our ability to learn. What questions have you been afraid of or desiring to ask of God? My heart is for you to feel the freedom to ask your questions and for you to renew your child-like sense of curiosity and wonder. God is big enough to handle any question you may have for Him. This is your permission to question.

Sorbe

Johnson and I are both learning how to question and let me tell you, it's been exciting to have permission to do so. It's a strange thing to consider, maybe, this "permission to question;" but, I would venture many of us struggle here in one form or another. Johnson and I are going to do our best to explain what

God has taught us–and continues to teach us–about questions and questioning. This is going to be fun!

My good friend, Jen (yes, another Jen in my life), sent me a text one day. We had been processing a confusing and uncomfortable situation. At the time, we were both looking to the Lord and each other to help find a resolution. Her text read one morning, "Hopefully one or more of us, by the Holy Spirit, will be able to identify when the devil is on the prowl. That is one of the lessons that I'm noting...this [issue] didn't come out of nowhere. I felt it in my heart, that he [the devil] was infiltrating, but I didn't know how to express it...I was blinded to the fact that we were battle buddies. I needed to ASK questions..."

She continued, "There is nothing wrong with asking questions! I must get that through my head. I'm scared and I'm new at it. Questioning is a skill that needs to be used often [for us] to get good at it, therefore, we then will have the ability to discern between the truth and the wiles of the devil."

Amen, Jen! I totally agree with you! There is nothing wrong with asking questions! How else are we going to learn? Since our early school days, we were taught that if we didn't know the answer, we should raise our hand and ask a question. Yet, I know people who have told me they were humiliated in front of class for asking a question just like Johnson stated above. For some, asking questions has been met with discipline, sarcasm, humiliation, or scolding. For those of you who have had negative experiences, asking questions is much harder for you to do. Asking questions makes you feel exposed in some way.

Here's a common one for me, "I'm sorry, could you tell me your name again?" This question scared me! I felt so embarrassed to ask this, so instead, I would have conversations without knowing the person's name. The longer it went on with me not knowing their name, the worse I felt. I have learned how to face this fear and now ask again if I have forgotten. In the end, I realized it was better for me to honor them by using their name as I spoke to them than to avoid asking. Little by little, I am coming out of my fear closet, and it is very freeing. I hope you will take these steps with us also.

> *"Ask and it will be given to you; seek and you will find; knock, and it will be opened to you. For everyone who asks receives, and the one who seeks finds, and to the one who knocks it will be opened."*
>
> Matthew 7:7-8 (NIV)

> *"If any of you lacks wisdom, let him ask God, who gives generously to all without reproach, and it will be given to him."*
>
> James 1:5 (NIV)

As I mentioned earlier, people ask questions for different reasons, or as Johnson says to me often, "from different heart places". One area I struggled to ask the right questions was in my marriage. Marriage is a place we could all use a little bit (or a lot) of help. The following example from my own marriage displays how my husband and I could have done better.

My husband came home from a business trip and observed the trash can overflowing. Within minutes of the excitement and hugs upon his arrival, in an exasperated voice he remarked to no one in particular, "Can't anyone see that the trash needs to be taken out?" As he grabbed the bag from the container, I heard a water bottle fall to the floor and then a soda can. I heard him breathe out a loud sigh, obviously annoyed. My skin prickled and my emotions began to match his. I was readying myself to defend my position. He had just stepped in as my enemy and I began to formulate a list in my mind of all I had been doing that week.

Besides, who does he think took the garbage out at least once already while he was away?!

His rhetorical question about the garbage revealed hidden emotions inside me and it led me straight to defensiveness. I was already feeling inadequate as a mother and a wife. Though I was doing all sorts of necessary things while he was away, I wasn't always doing them well. I felt like there weren't enough hours in the day to get it all done. His exasperated question about the garbage reminded me of my own perceived shortcomings and his statement poked a growing insecurity. *Doesn't he see what I do for our family? He doesn't appreciate me!* I began to pull from past, unresolved hurts that were cataloged in my mind to quantify my growing hurt and anger towards him and add them to this latest infraction. Little did he know, I was allowing his flippant statement to cut so deep. In his own mind, he had expectations about how the house would look when he got home. His unspoken expectations grew into frustration each time he saw them unmet, and he felt disrespected because of it.

Let's dig a little deeper and break this scenario down. My husband came home and asked a rhetorical question out of frustration. He chose to indirectly deal with an issue that bothered him, not realizing the negative impact it would have on my emotions. On the other hand, I avoided asking him questions that would clarify why he was so frustrated with the trash. Because I chose not to get clarification, I was unable to understand why he was frustrated and applied it as a direct assault to my abilities, making him look way worse in my mind. Because he chose to react to the garbage and not invest in a meaningful conversation, by asking questions, as to how my week went while he was away, he missed knowing where my heart stood. Because I took his question as a personal attack, I didn't have the capacity to care about his feelings; in fact, I would have dismissed them entirely with that state of mind. We each formed our own conclusions based on assumptions. We were missing the mark.

Johnson

Sorbe! I am taking notes. Underlining the above section and joking about getting a tattoo of your marriage advice. So convicted right now, in the absolute best way!

Sorbe

Asking questions can prevent conflict. It helps us find the "why" behind the statement or the action (or lack of action), giving us more information to work with and thus removing assumptions. It may take some practice, but over time it can be a very helpful tool for keeping a miscommunication from turning into a fight. Getting to know the way someone else thinks and perceives situations can really open your heart to understanding them better, while saving you from jumping to conclusions by operating within your own assumptions. Our assumptions are rarely correct. They often come from a perspective derived from a negative memory. It's better to get the truth from the person directly in order to formulate your conclusions. Keep asking questions and encouraging the other person to ask theirs as well. Hugs to all of you going through tough times in marriage. Good communication is worth learning more about![1] Believe me, we could all use a little more training–me included!

Questions can come out of a place of desperation, or they can be used as an invitation for further reflection, in order to ponder deeper things. In Mark 4:35-41, we come to the story where Jesus and his disciples are traveling by sea. Jesus slept as they sailed; a windstorm developed and hit the boat hard. So overwhelming was the storm hitting their boat, that this group of once-fishermen were terrified they would surely die. They ran to Jesus and shook him awake, crying, "Teacher, do you not care that we are perishing?!" Jesus woke up and rebuked the wind and the raging waves and immediately they ceased. It says the disciples were both afraid and it notes that they marveled. In other words, they were marvelously afraid. Yes, I would be too! In one moment, they were being swallowed up by water and in the next moment, experienced peace.

HE WANTS US TO TRUST IN HIM, NOT OURSELVES.

Did you notice in their panicked state they went to Jesus, albeit accusatory? I think this is worthy of consideration. What do you do in a panicked state? Is your first inclination to go to Jesus, even if it's to blame Him for your stormy trials? God wants us to rely on Him, to trust Him, and to invite Him into all situations. I quote Proverbs 3:5-6 often. "Trust in the Lord with all your heart, lean not on your own understanding. In all your ways acknowledge Him and He will make your paths straight." He wants us to trust in Him, not ourselves. The disciples were learning this lesson, just like you and I. There is something even deeper to learn here–trusting in the faithfulness of Jesus. In 1 Thessalonians 5:24 we read, "The One Who called you is faithful and will do what He promised." Jesus does what He promises He will do.

My buddy Joe said to me one day, "There's a difference between asking questions and questioning." So right you are, Joe. And like Johnson says, it depends on the heart behind the question. I view these as connecting statements. When my first-born son was in his elementary years, he questioned everything. Most of the time it was because he was so inquisitive about how things worked and simply wanted to know more. Sometimes, his questions were because he didn't want to do what I asked of him. So, as I refused to be the "because I told you so" mom, I allowed him 4 questions. I would honestly and decisively answer his questions as to the rationale for my request. After those 4 questions were answered, if he still did not do as I asked, it was disobedience. You see, he had been given all the information he needed to do what I had asked of him. I knew I was a loving and rational mother and would not ask him to do something immoral or seek to bring him hardship. So, if he chose to continue asking me questions, I knew he did not want to obey and was either stalling or challenging my authority.

> *"Or which one of you, if his son asks him for bread, will give him a stone? Or if he asks for a fish, will give him a serpent? If you then, who are evil, know how to give good gifts to your children, how much more will your Father who is in heaven give good things to those who ask him!"*
>
> Matthew 7:9-11 (ESV)

It's time to step into our purpose and into obedience. Obedience places us in our purpose. It may start with questions in our prayer time, but it shouldn't stay there. There comes a time when the questions have been asked and we must step out in obedience to what God is calling us to do. Maybe He's calling you to forgive someone who has hurt you in the past, or to humble yourself and apologize for something. Maybe He's calling you to write a book, even though you don't feel qualified. Maybe He's calling you to start a Bible study in your home and invite your neighbor. Regardless of the calling, He loves you and wants to set your feet on solid ground. He does not fear your questions; you have His permission to ask them. You only then need to open your ears to listen and truly hear His answers to step out into obedience.

> *"For I know the plans I have for you," declares the Lord, "plans to prosper you and not to harm you, plans to give you hope and a future. Then you will call on me and come and pray to me, and I will listen to you. You will seek me and find me when you seek me with all your heart."*
>
> Jeremiah 29:11-13 (NIV)

Johnson

"People look at the outward appearance but the Lord looks at the heart" (Samuel16:7b). God knows the heart of why we are asking Him things. Just like Sorbe knew the reasons behind her son asking so many questions, his desire was not to get more information so he could do the job better; rather, it was to get out of doing what he had been asked to do. Are you stalling and making excuses, or seeking direction, wisdom, and understanding?

In Matthew 19:16-22, we are presented with an example of someone who asked Jesus an important question, but he did not personally apply the answer to his life. This story is our next example of stupid, but I feel a little harsh giving this young man that designation. But again, whenever God tells us to do something and we do not do it, it is ultimately stupid. As you read through his story, study the questions and write down any observations you find. Also feel free to ask your own questions. Questions help us to move past the superficial level using scripture and dig deeper.

You have permission to question.

> *Another day, a man stopped Jesus and asked, "Teacher, what good thing must I do to get eternal life?"*

> *Jesus said, "Why do you question me about what is good? God is the One who is good. If you want to enter the life of God, just do what he tells you."*
>
> *The man asked, "What in particular?"*
>
> *Jesus said, "Don't murder, don't commit adultery, don't steal, don't lie, honor your father and mother, and love your neighbor as yourself."*
>
> *The young man said, "I've done all that. What's left?"*
>
> *"If you want to give it all you've got," Jesus replied, "go sell your possessions; give everything to the poor. All your wealth will then be in heaven. Then come follow me."*
>
> *That was the last thing the young man expected to hear. And so, crestfallen, he walked away. He was holding on tight to a lot of things, and he couldn't bear to let go.*
>
> Matthew 19:16-22 (MSG)

What basic observations can be made from reading this story? One answer is that there is a difference between being good and being perfect. Following the commandments gives life, but following Jesus gives eternal life. That God is the only one who is truly good. That Jesus both answered people and He also asked questions. Answering questions is how we reveal if we have really heard and processed the information.

What questions could we ask to dig deeper into this story? Here are some examples of questions my daughter Zoey and I came up with. "What do I still lack? Would I feel comfortable asking Jesus the same questions the young man in the story did? Do you feel Jesus was asking too much from the young man? Did the disciples have to give up everything to follow Jesus? What things are people willing to give up everything for? What other times are 'good' and 'perfect' used in the Bible?"

Learning how to actively question is an important part of our *trust the process* journey. Asking these kinds of questions will help you to really engage fully with what you are reading versus simply rushing through it. When we fail to ask questions, we will miss out on the fullness of what God has for us in the Bible.

The questions the young man asked Jesus were good questions. From an external human perspective, it looked like his desire was to do more than merely meet the basic "requirements." He wanted more. The truth was he wasn't looking for a relationship with Christ. He wanted Jesus to give him a religious rule to follow, one he could fulfill on his own without the need of a Savior.

I learned a practical way to seek God with my questions from a respected member of my family–my Uncle Doug. He is a math and science professional, and a great example of a noble questioner. Whenever he has a question, he writes it down and puts it in a designated box. Over the years, he has asked God some very complex intellectual questions. Some of these inquiries are answered right away; others have taken a few months or even up to a year, but God always leads him to the right answer. Answers would come as he read the Bible, had conversations with friends, read random books, or heard a Sunday sermon. As soon as he had the opportunity, he would go to his box of questions and pull out the correct card. Then he would write the answer down on the paper and place it into a new box.

Did the disciples have to give up everything to follow Jesus? Yes. What things are people willing to give up everything for? A trip to outer space maybe?

Did you know that right now you can book a trip to outer space for approximately $250,000? This may seem like a crazy amount of money to some people but is viewed as a once in a lifetime opportunity to others. People will give up everything for opportunity, romantic relationships, even a bowl of soup (Esau, Jacob's twin brother). It all depends on what you value. Peter was asked by Jesus to leave his job to follow Him...and Peter responded by dropping his fishing net. He quit his job immediately. That decision led him to become the first fisherman to step out of his boat and walk on water. These men exchanged their common lives for front row seats to events that changed the course of history. They traded their earthly breakable stuff for a taste of Heaven. They watched Jesus mend and heal the broken things in this world. They witnessed the dead being brought back to life. The disciples were taught by the greatest teacher this world has ever known. Many people will give more than what they have, to be taught by a respected teacher...it is called college. How many of us will not even flinch at going into debt for a car, a house, or a 50% off sale? This world *demands* more than what you have. Jesus, though, takes your garbage stuff and He washes your feet. He gives you, His inheritance. He ultimately gives us everything in exchange for our nothing. After processing this question with you, I can now say with full confidence...my heart breaks for the young man. He missed out on the greatest opportunity of his life; he walked away from his answer. He understood that Jesus was the one he should bring his questions to, but he was unable to fully receive the answer.

HIS PERMISSION TO QUESTION IS A LIFELONG GIFT.

Here is what we can learn from this man's sad story: Don't walk away, take your questions to Jesus and trust He will respond with great wisdom. As you seek and receive, be prepared for Him to encourage you, push you beyond intellect into spiritual growth, and call you to some course of action. His permission to question is a lifelong gift; and, if used with the right heart, will become a natural part of your back-and-forth communication with

Jesus. He wants you to trust Him with every one of your questions and know that His answers are more than simply good–they are perfect.

Group Discussion Questions/Action Step/ Personal Reflection/Journal:

- How did Holy Spirit speak to you as you read through chapter 8?

- What are your personal reasons for asking God questions? Are you stalling or desiring to know more about God and His plans for your life?

- What questions do you have for God? Pray and seek the Lord for an answer.

Assignment: Read a chapter in the Bible, write down the first question that comes to mind. Write down what you find?

Prayer

Dear Jesus, I long to bring You my questions. I trust You will lead me to satisfying answers. Prepare my heart to respond to You in obedience.

In Jesus' name, amen.

NO FEAR

"I am not alone. Who is the One who is always with me? My Protector, my Heavenly Father, my Shelter, the one who keeps my feet from slipping. This is why we do not fear, because we know the One whom the wind and the waves obey. The One who stands in the fire with us and protects even our clothes from the smell of smoke."
Johnson

"Be sober [well balanced and self-disciplined], be alert and cautious at all times. That enemy of yours, the devil, prowls around like a roaring lion [fiercely hungry], seeking someone to devour. But resist him, be firm in your faith [against his attack—rooted, established, immovable], knowing that the same experiences of suffering are being experienced by your brothers and sisters throughout the world. [You do not suffer alone.]
1 Peter 5:8-9 (AMP)

Fear: noun
An unpleasant emotion caused by the belief that someone or something is dangerous, likely to cause pain, or a threat.

9–KILLING FEAR

Courage is knowing what not to fear.
Plato

"Success is not final, failure is not fatal: it is the courage to continue that counts."
Winston S. Churchill

Johnson

"Have I not commanded you? Be strong and courageous! Do not tremble or be dismayed, for the Lord your God is with you wherever you go."

Joshua 1:9 (NIV)

Let's get some things straight before we dive into spiritual warfare. Evil is real. Satan is real. Demons are real, and Hell is absolutely, 100% real. But thankfully, so is Heaven, God, Jesus, and the Holy Spirit. We find a lot of encouragement by combining the NASB, KJV, and BLB versions of the Bible to get a full picture of what God has for us in 2 Timothy 1:17. This is to give you a small taste of what God has planned for you in this chapter: No Fear. Please take your time and think on each word placed in this powerful verse from 2 Timothy.

"For God has not given us a spirit of fear and timidity, but of power, love, and self-discipline."

2 Timothy 1:7 (NLT)

God is planning on removing every spirit of timidity, cowardice, and fear from your life. You have already learned how to listen to God and open yourself up to His plans. Your faith is growing as you trust the process; now it is time to put these spiritual disciplines into practice. This may sound crazy, fun, or even stupid, but God says in His word that all things are possible through Him. He has even commanded us to not be afraid. Believe me, you absolutely want to be courageous–this is something that God longs to give you! Being fearless will make you a true warrior, ready to do everything God is asking of you; this may include, but is not limited to, God nudging us to offer doughnuts to strangers, like my very real experience in chapter 4.

Sorbe

Thank you for that intro, Johnson. "Being fearless will make you a true warrior." We think fear helps us, but it doesn't. "Yeah, but Sorbe, isn't some fear healthy to have? Doesn't it keep us from doing something dangerous?" Let's take a moment to unpack this idea with a personal story.

Having been in Texas all week, my family and I are headed back to our home in Wisconsin and stop halfway to sleep at a hotel. Early the next morning I wake up before everyone else and decide to put in my earbuds and listen to worship music. I feel the Holy Spirit move in my heart and I quietly worship God and thank Him for all my blessings.

It was time to shower and prepare to leave. I grab a change of clothes out of my suitcase, along with a hat to cover up my messy hair. It'll just be another day of driving anyway. I set my clothes and hat onto the counter and step into the shower. My thoughts are all with God as I pray about several things on my mind. I dry off and pick my hat up off my jeans and scream. A 4.5-inch Giant Hairy Scorpion scurries across my folded jeans. I jump back, protected by nothing but the skin God gave me and immediately begin to consider the ways to deal with this thing without getting stung! Was it going to jump at me? Do I put it into the garbage? The toilet? Hit it with a shoe? I command my mind to think rationally as I keep my eyes on it. I'm from the cold Midwest. We do not have scorpions. I have no point of reference besides some Discovery Channel documentary where I observed a scorpion stabbing its prey.

My eldest son has heard my scream. I get my PJs back on and open the door and point to what caused me to cry out. He stepped back. "Lord, you have given me the power to tread on scorpions!" I yell.[1] Steadying my hands, I gingerly pick up my jeans with this Texas hitchhiker settled upon them, flip it over into the toilet and flush it down!

Danger now averted and taking a moment to breathe, I contemplate my next move. I needed to get dressed but now I was afraid to put on my jeans. I stare at them and imagine four more scorpions dropping out onto the floor scurrying towards my feet. I declare passionately that there is no way I am putting those jeans on now! My son counters, "Oh, yes you will mom! No fear!" My shoulders drop, acknowledging the truth of his statement. If I didn't deal with this fear right away, it was going to take me captive and own me. Every time I picked up folded jeans, I would relive this fear I was experiencing right now. I hear 2 Corinthians 10:5 roll through my mind, "Take all your thoughts captive under the obedience of Christ" and then 2 Timothy 1:7: "I have not been given a spirit of fear." So, despite my emotions attempting to control me, I choose to stand on God's truth and unfold my jeans boldly. No more scorpions came out and I got dressed. Fear did not win, though for several days after that I had to go to those verses to keep my brain from submitting to it. Eventually I began envisioning myself picking up a scorpion by the tail without fear. Thank You, Jesus.

FEAR DOES NOT RESIDE IN HEAVEN.

Yeah, but can we really be fearless? What does God say about it? Proverbs 3:5 says, "Trust in the Lord with all your heart and lean not unto your own understanding." What scripture did Johnson quote just a moment ago? 2 Timothy 1:7: "For God has not given us the spirit of fear." Fear does not reside in heaven. So, where does it reside if not in heaven? On earth. Fallen, sinful, earth that is "ruled" by the king of this world–the devil. Did God plant that scorpion there? No way! The Bible says that God is a good father. A good father would not place a scorpion on my pants to harm me. Matthew 7:11 says, "If you then, who are evil, know how to give good gifts to your children, how much more will your Father who is in heaven give good things to those who ask Him." But I do know who does want me destroyed. In John chapter 10 we read about a 'father' who does want to destroy us: the father of lies, the false shepherd, the thief, the accuser. Satan and all the angels who followed him were cast out of heaven. "And He said to them, 'I saw satan fall like lightning from heaven.'"[2] Regarding satan and his demons, we are told in scripture, "The thief comes ONLY to steal and kill and destroy. I came that they may have life and have it abundantly." Jesus continues, "I am the good shepherd. The good shepherd lays down his life for the sheep." (John 10:10-11, emphasis mine). "Behold, I give you the authority to trample on serpents and scorpions, and over all the power of the enemy, and nothing shall by any means hurt you" (Luke 10:19 ESV). So, where does fear come from? That's right. The devil. Therefore, we do not want it nor should we accept it.

I had a Zombie Dream that called me to action. Have any of you ever thought about zombies? I have. I grew up watching sci-fi shows with my dad. I love fantasy movies, action movies, and movies about survival. It would be no wonder, then, that God chose to use zombies to speak to me. Imagine, if you will, a quaint 50's style town with sweet little shops on both sides of Main Street. There's a church on the corner with stairs rising up to red double doors. A steeple rises from the roof above the doors and is mounted with a cross. No one is in the town, save for myself, Johnson, and all our young children. It's daylight and nothing seems to be scary or off except for what we are about to have our children do. We were going to be sending them inside the church. Johnson and I know that inside that quaint little church on the corner there are a bunch of zombies aimlessly walking around. What was once hallowed ground is now seething with death and destruction, looking for those they can devour. Outside the church, we are standing with our children about to dispatch what is most precious to us directly into that pit of hell. Our precious little souls will be stepping inside, and we would not be going with them. The battle will be theirs and theirs alone.

As they climb the steps and enter the double doors, I look to Johnson and ask if they will make it out alive. She turned to me and affirmed, "What we have trained them to do will have to be enough. The rest is up to them. We cannot do it for them." With concern for what the outcome will be, I watch as the last child steps into the darkness. The door shuts behind them; and, as soon as the door closed, I awoke from the dream. I tried as hard as I could to go back to sleep and recreate the moment where I saw my children exit on the back side of that church alive. But as hard as I tried, I could not create a new ending. I am crying as I type this because that dream still feels so very real to me. I prayed to God then, as I continue to pray now, for wisdom to raise my children ready for battle. A battle that will surround them whether they are ready for it or not. Will I have taught them well enough? Well, I am not going to sit around and hope for the best...I am going to do something about it and train them for battle.

> *"For though we walk in the flesh, we are not waging war according to the flesh. For the weapons of our warfare are not of the flesh but have divine power to destroy* ***strongholds****. We destroy arguments and every lofty opinion raised against the knowledge of God and take every thought captive to obey Christ."*
>
> 2 Corinthians 10:3-6 (ESV)

We are skin and bone, but we are being told in these verses that our war is not against other humans. We are at war with the devil and his demons. The above verse says we have divine power to destroy strongholds! Many Christians don't even know they have this power. It is power which comes from the Holy Spirit, also known as the Helper[3]; we receive the Holy Spirit when we ask Jesus to save us from our sins. Remember, Jesus told the disciples, in John 14:12, "I tell you for certain that if you have faith in me, you will do the same things I am doing. You will do even greater things, now that I am going back to the Father." When Jesus left earth to be seated at the right hand of the Father, we gained the highest position of authority, in His name, with which to defeat the devil.

Let's talk about strongholds. A stronghold is a place that has been fortified so as to protect whatever is behind it against attack. In Psalm 9:9, we read that the Lord is a stronghold for the oppressed, a stronghold in times of trouble. In Jeremiah 16:19, the Lord is our strength and our stronghold and our refuge. I love how God is our stronghold! Think about it this way–He is strong, and He is holding on to us. That is very comforting and emboldening.

Contrary to God's loving and protective strongholds, the enemy builds them too. As we read above in 2 Corinthians 10:3, our spiritual weapons have the divine power to *destroy* strongholds. The strongholds discussed in this verse are the devil's. Our thoughts about money, sex, marriage, humanity, and more can have strongholds built around them, but *who* built those strongholds is what really matters. Are they strongholds rooted in Christ or are they strongholds cemented in our minds by the enemy?

"Don't let anyone under pressure to give in to evil say, "God is trying to trip me up." God is impervious to evil, and

puts evil in no one's way. The temptation to give in to evil comes from us and only us. We have no one to blame but the leering, seducing flare-up of our own lust. Lust gets pregnant, and has a baby: sin! Sin grows up to adulthood, and becomes a real killer. So, my very dear friends, don't get thrown off course. Every desirable and beneficial gift comes out of heaven. The gifts are rivers of light cascading down from the Father of Light. There is nothing deceitful in God, nothing two-faced, nothing fickle. He brought us to life using the true Word, showing us off as the crown of all His creatures."

James 1:13-18 (MSG)

FIRST ORDER OF BUSINESS IS TO PUT ON THE WHOLE ARMOR OF GOD.

Throughout our lives, we build a worldview based on our experiences and what we've been taught. If our worldview is based on anything but a Godly perspective, it has the ability to keep us from walking fully in our identity in Christ. When the enemy whispers to us and we do not resist him, strongholds begin to take form. Knowingly or unknowingly, we let them manifest and take root. Many of these strongholds get built around the lies we believe. God has given us the power to tear down these strongholds of the enemy. My friends, our Hope is in the Lord. The first order of business is to put on the whole armor of God.

"Finally, be strong in the Lord and in the strength of his might. Put on the whole armor of God, that you may be able to stand against the schemes of the devil. ***For we***

> ***do not wrestle against flesh and blood, but against the rulers, against the authorities, against the cosmic powers over this present darkness, against the spiritual forces of evil in the heavenly places.*** *Therefore take up the whole armor of God, that you may be able to withstand in the evil day, and having done all, to stand firm. Stand therefore, having fastened on the belt of truth, and having put on the breastplate of righteousness, and, as shoes for your feet, having put on the readiness given by the gospel of peace. In all circumstances take up the shield of faith, with which you can extinguish all the flaming darts of the evil one; and take the helmet of salvation, and the sword of the Spirit, which is the word of God, praying at all times in the Spirit, with all prayer and supplication. To that end, keep alert with all perseverance, making supplication for all the saints."*
>
> Ephesians 6:10-18 (ESV)

So, in this word from God we are told our battle is not against flesh and blood, right? We must be armed for battle. We must use spiritual armor and spiritual weapons to fight this war. In my dream, above, I mentioned zombies. Zombies are often referred to as the "walking dead." They look for anything alive to devour.

I view satan as the king of the walking dead. Satan, once a beautiful angel in heaven, rebelled against his own God created identity. You see, he wanted to *be* God rather than to *serve* God; and, because of his rebellion, he was thrown out of heaven.[4] Now he spends his days and nights prowling around, looking for people to devour. I Peter 5:8 warns us to "be sober-minded; be watchful. Your adversary the devil prowls around like a roaring lion, seeking someone to devour." The enemy wants to devour mankind. Sounds very zombie-like to me. Because we are made in the very image of God[5], we are hated by satan.

THE ENEMY'S GREATEST TACTIC TO COMBAT GOD IS THROUGH THE DESTRUCTION OF WHAT GOD LOVES MOST–US.

The enemy's greatest tactic to combat God is through the destruction of what God loves most–us. Though there is no need for us to be afraid of him, we do need to know how to protect ourselves from his attacks. In 1 John 4:4 we are told, "Little children, you are from God and have overcome them [evil spirits], for He who is in you is greater than he who is in the world." So instead of us being overcome–spiritual bondage–we can be the overcomers! We do not need to listen to these spirits of the world for they speak worldly things. Once saved, we become new creations in Christ Jesus.[6] Though our bodies stay the same, our Spirit is now indwelt with the Holy Spirit. What was once empty and void is now filled with the light of Christ! We now have the authority to tell the devil to leave us alone. Though he may come at us again and again, we have all the power to resist and defeat him!

> "The seventy-two returned with joy, saying, 'Lord, even the demons are subject to us in your name!' And he said to them, 'I saw satan fall like lightning from heaven. Behold, I have given you authority to tread on serpents and scorpions, and over all the power of the enemy, and nothing shall hurt you. Nevertheless, do not rejoice in this, that the spirits are subject to you, but rejoice that your names are written in heaven.'"
>
> Luke 10:17-20 (ESV)

God has already told us we are at war. He has instructed us to put on our armor and stand firm. Ephesians 6 guides us to "be strong in the Lord and in the strength of his might." We have something this king of death does not have–the power of the Holy Spirit Himself, living in us–and in Him we have all power to defeat this enemy and destroy those fortified walls.

How do we put this into practice? We submit to God. We pray. We praise. We worship. We love. We rebuke. We fast. We forgive.[7] I'll let you in on something: satan is the antithesis of God. God *cannot* lie; satan *always* lies.[8]

Do you know why God's way seems so crazy and stupid to us? It's because we are being deceived to believe God's way is stupid. If we are not battle-ready, we will be easily deceived. There was a wonderful pastor at a church I attended in Colorado in my twenties who would often say, "If you believe in nothing, you will fall for anything." What is belief anyway? It is faith or acceptance that a statement is true or that something exists.[9]

All around us there are businesses selling us their goods, telling us their product will solve any given problem. Do you believe them? What skills do you use to decide if what they say is worth believing? How many times have you purchased something only to find out it doesn't live up to its promise? Did you know, in 2018 there was a recorded 283 billion dollars spent in the US on advertising?[10] That number is rising every year. There must be something valuable in advertising if there is that much money being thrown at it. We know it works because we are the ones consuming it.

Much like these advertisers, satan knows he can "sell" us his goods too. He's a great marketer... feeding on our weakness, our boredom, our desires in order to lure us towards his perversion of God's truth. You see, if we are not grounded in God's truth, we will fall easily for his deceptions. The entirety of the world around us speaks for him in different ways. He perverts love into abuse.

He perverts hard work into obsession. He perverts financial gain into the love of money. He perverts forgiveness into self-righteous indignation. He perverts enjoying food into gluttony. He perverts health into self-loathing or self-worshiping. He perverts friendship with your children into control and rebellion. The list goes on. In order to protect our minds from this deception, we must know our identity IN CHRIST or we will fall prey to his perversions and accept them as truth. Not only do we need to know who we are in Christ, we need to know whose we are. The only way we can begin to understand who we are in Christ, is to study God's word and see what God says about who we are to Him and who He is to us.

One of my cousins called me a while back to share a very concerning dream she had one night. In the dream, she was being murdered and she woke up screaming. Two nights later, her husband had a similar dream and woke up the same way. This shook her to her core, and she reached out to me to talk about it. It came time for us to pray and I declared safety over her life in Jesus' name; but for some reason, I felt like she needed to be the one to pray. As she began, I heard, "Ask her who do I (God) say she is?". I had to ask the question twice before she responded with what was one of the most powerful replies I had ever heard her utter: "I am the daughter of the most high God." She said it with such certainty it brought tears to my eyes, and I knew the enemy had no power over her anymore. Her prayer after that pronouncement flowed out like a river of power and fire. It. Was. Awesome.

We are told we [born-again believers] are aliens in this world.[11] We are to be in the world but not of the world.[12]

> *"Friends, this world is not your home, so don't make yourselves cozy in it. Don't indulge your ego at the expense of your soul. Live an exemplary life among the*

natives so that your actions will refute their prejudices. Then they'll be won over to God's side and be there to join in the celebration when he arrives."

1 Peter 2:11-12 (MSG)

"Do not love the world or the things in the world. If anyone loves the world, the love of the Father is not in him. For all that is in the world—the desires of the flesh and the desires of the eyes and pride of life- is not from the Father but is from the world. And the world is passing away along with its desires, but whoever does the will of God abides forever. Children, it is the last hour, and as you have heard that antichrist is coming, so now many antichrists have come. Therefore we know that it is the last hour. They went out from us, but they were not of us; for if they had been of us, they would have continued with us. But they went out, that it might become plain that they all are not of us."

1 John 2:15-19 (ESV)

"You're cheating on God. If all you want is your own way, flirting with the world every chance you get, you end up enemies of God and his way. And do you suppose God doesn't care? The proverb has it that "he's a fiercely jealous lover." And what he gives in love is far better than anything else you'll find. It's common knowledge that "God goes against the willful proud; God gives grace to the willing humble."

James 4:4-6 (MSG)

"And that about wraps it up. God is strong, and he wants you strong. So take everything the Master has set out for you, well-made weapons of the best materials. And put

> *them to use so you will be able to stand up to everything the Devil throws your way. This is no weekend war that we'll walk away from and forget about in a couple of hours. This is for keeps, a life-or-death fight to the finish against the Devil and all his angels."*
>
> Ephesians 6:10-12 (MSG)

What lies have you believed only to finally wake up to the truth and feel fooled? We've all been there. As I mentioned before, the battle is not against flesh, but against spiritual forces. These forces, whether you want to believe they exist or not, are real. We must be battle-trained and prepared to deal with them effectively.

Satan uses many avenues to deceive us. Sometimes, it can be a well-meaning friend distracting you from your mission. In Matthew 16:22-23, Jesus is telling the disciples he would soon die. Peter, one of those chosen men, takes Jesus aside and begins to rebuke him. Can you even imagine?! Doesn't Peter know by now what Jesus says is going to happen... always happens? In this instance, however, Peter is thinking with his emotional brain. He reacts to this new information with a rebuke to Jesus, the King of kings, and argues, "Far be it from you, Lord! This shall never happen to you."

Now, we all know Jesus came into this world for this exact reason. He came to die as the final perfect sacrifice for our sin, a blood covering that is everlasting to those who choose to believe and accept His sacrifice. What if Jesus had listened to Peter? All hope would have been lost and satan would have won the entire war. The reality was Peter didn't like what he heard Jesus say. He thought it was stupid and he wasn't going to stay quiet about it. It may be easy to judge Peter here, but that news was no doubt very shocking. I can imagine that the thought of going on without Jesus by their side was not something they wanted to entertain.

I can see myself making the same mistake as Peter; and, though Jesus' response seems harsh, he loved Peter very much–so much that he didn't allow him to be used by the devil. Jesus turns to Peter and says, "Get behind me, satan! You are a hindrance to me. For you are not setting your mind on the things of God, but the things of man." It seems so awful, but think about it thoroughly. In the first part of His response to Peter, Jesus rebukes not Peter, but satan, himself. I believe the second part was meant for Peter, reminding him to set his mind heavenward. Jesus knew when it was satan speaking vs God speaking, and He dealt with it swiftly–calling it out directly. I'm sure this shocked Peter. He certainly would not have *intended* to be used as the enemy's mouthpiece! But sadly, in that instance, it is exactly what he was.

How did Jesus know it was satan speaking through Peter and not just Peter, as a friend, trying to encourage Him or stand up for Him? Because Jesus knew the voice of God and He followed it. Jesus calls us His sheep and says if we know His voice, we will follow it. An interesting thing about sheep is they will not come to a stranger's call. In fact, they don't even pay any attention to someone else's voice at all. But, if they hear their shepherd's voice, the one whom they know, they will come running. I recently viewed videos of this phenomena online and I was amazed how the truth of this scripture played out in the natural world.

> *"When he has brought out all his own, he goes before them, for they know his voice. A stranger they will not follow, but they will flee from him, for they do not know the voice of strangers."*
>
> John 10:4-5 (ESV)

Jesus knows words have power, meaning and intention. There are 31 verses I can find concerning words and their power. When you know the voice of God, you will not be deceived by any other voice. Jesus actively prayed, sought after God the Father, fasted, and rested. He did this regularly. He was well-armed and thus could not be deceived. You may say, "Well, that's easy for Him–He's God." We know Jesus chose to submit to the Father's will and allow the Holy Spirit to flow through him when he came down to little ol' earth to live like one of us. We have the same opportunity to live like Jesus did! We read over and over that Jesus would go off to pray. If Jesus felt the need to pray, then we should too.

Scripture tells us " the Word became flesh and dwelt among us."[13] Jesus was born into the world like us. He lived like us. He ate like us, was cold like us, hungry like us, and happy like us; "and being found in human form, he humbled himself by becoming obedient to the point of death."[14] As to what Jesus was willing to put aside in order to come alongside us–his deity and all its power–even though many didn't listen...now that's true love. That, my friends, is humble, active love like nothing else and no one else. Jesus is our go-to. He's our how-to, our cornerstone.... our example. He is our "do." He is the only voice we should be listening to, because He always has our best interests at heart. Being a sheep to Him? Well, that's wisdom. Being a sheep to the world and the devil? That's just plain stupid.

Let me say one more thing about being one of Jesus' sheep. When one sheep is lost, He will leave the rest to go find the one. Read Luke 15:4-7. Let me make this a little more personal. Let's say you have three children and one goes missing. What would you do? I can guess what I would do at a bare minimum. I would call everyone I knew and ask them to call everyone they knew to help me find my missing child. I'd call the police and the newspapers. I wouldn't eat or sleep. I wouldn't stop looking. No cost would be too great to find him! But when I find my missing child...oh, can you imagine?! Tears of joy, unspeakable! Can you envision the celebration you, your friends, family, and neighbors would have? Likely, even strangers who were walking this road with you would cry in celebration and relief! This is how–and much more–our Lord and His angels in heaven feel about a lost person being saved. Wow!

> *"Count on it–there's more joy in heaven over one sinner's rescued life than over ninety-nine good people in no need of rescue."*
>
> Luke 15:7 (MSG)

Johnson

> *"Give me one hundred preachers who fear nothing but sin and desire nothing but God, and I care not whether they be clergymen or laymen, they alone will shake the gates of Hell and set up the kingdom of Heaven upon Earth."*
>
> John Wesley

At this moment, I am humbled. This battle we are engaged in is not an easy one. There is a reason why we are called to daily put on the full armor of God, to pray without ceasing, because we are in a very real, ever-present war. God is pushing and challenging me as I write these words, making me very uncomfortable. The reason for my nerves and my blushing face is because I need to confess something to you. I just had another Lot moment. Yep–I am writing a book about obeying God immediately, not choosing the stupid path, and here I am not practicing the very thing He is teaching me. God is calling me to lay my heart bare before you. He is calling me to a level of transparency to which I am uncomfortable. This is the conversation I am having with God right now. "God, why couldn't you have me write a book where I could talk about all my successes? All the times I did it right?" God's response, "Because, Jenny, I am glorified in your frailty, not your strengths. This book is not meant to point people to you, but to me. Lean on me and I will give you the strength needed to accomplish what I have asked of you."

In High School, I engaged in a dating relationship that was broken, abusive, and disobedient. I chose to enter and stay far too long in this relationship, knowing God was screaming for me to disengage. I had trusted God with many other areas of my life, but not this one. The truth was, I really wasn't supposed to date in high school. God had called me into ministry. There was a group of amazing junior high girls I was meeting with regularly to fellowship with and mentor. I had written a series of plays with my best friend from high school, which we performed at our church. God had called me to be a writer and a teacher. He had laid such a beautiful plan before me, so why did I not trust him? Simple. I believed a lie from the enemy, and I used it to make pitiful excuses before God. I was afraid that by God saying not now, it would mean not ever. I just wanted to be like everybody else. Satan whispered, "Jenny, no one will ever be attracted to you. You are undesirable. If you listen to God, you will end up alone. You will always be 'JUST JENNY.'"

"Just Jenny'' was spoken over me in Junior High by my best guy friend. Most summer days I would walk over to his house, knock on his door, and off we would go on any number of outdoor adventures. Perhaps, we would walk down to Lake Superior to swim, buy blue raspberry suckers at the gas station, venture off to a nearby country club to hunt for stray golf balls, hike at Lester Park, or watch my friend jump off the train bridge and into the river. As much time as we spent together, the thought of dating never entered my mind, until the day someone teased us about liking each other. I watched my close childhood friend make a grossed-out face and he said, "Eww...no. She's Jenny, just Jenny." He was like a brother to me, and I understood what he meant, but internally I thought, "What is wrong with me? Maybe, I will always be *Just Jenny*."

This lie of 'Just Jenny' morphed into a far more dangerous belief. "Jenny, no one will ever be attracted to you. You are undesirable and you will always be *Just Jenny*." These words formed a very real hole in my armor. Enter in temptation–a boy from a respected Christian family, desired by countless girls, played the guitar, and carried enough obvious pain to grab my attention. The devil was handing me poison and I drank it. I entered into this dangerous relationship because I wanted to help him. I was flattered by his advancements, and I was no longer "alone." I thought I knew so much better than God, but oh, how very wrong I was. Here is a quote from this ex-boyfriend, sent in a sincere apology letter many years later. I believe it shows exactly what the enemy was bringing into my life and how it went against everything God had planned for me: "I was intentionally trying to hurt you, at least the first summer when we dated. I remember hating your innocence, despising you trying to help me, and taking it as a personal challenge to corrupt you."

This is what the devil's plans for us look like. He hates everything that resembles Christ in you. He hates your innocence, he is actively trying to hurt you, and his greatest desire is to corrupt and soil you. Now that we have gotten a glimpse at the enemy, we are going to go deeper.

Enter my Lot moment number 2. I was incredibly excited to have a night alone in a hotel to work on this book. I love having designated time to listen to the Holy Spirit, feeling His presence, and doing the very thing for which He has purposed me. I had just started writing, finished up the story about the plane, when I heard God say, "Next, tell them about your dream." My exact thought? "Nope. That is not going to happen."

I ignored God and continued to read what Sorbe had written, and at the very end of her powerful message, she had left a note for me–"Jenny, put your dream here." I got goosebumps all over. What?! Seriously, God. Wow. I called my editor and she again confirmed what God was telling me. I told her about the dream, and she said, "Jenny, do you need to hear it a third time? You need to put your dream in the book."

Okay, so here are my excuses. I do really feel justified in my fears. Of course, I know I am being a big baby, just like I called Moses a big man baby. Maybe he really was a terrible public speaker! Having some real empathy for Moses, right now. Anyway, regarding my reasons–they're actually not reasons. A more accurate description would be the devil's lies to dissuade me. A voice whispers, "Jenny, if you write about a supernatural dream, what will people think? I'll tell you what they will think. You are bonkers, that is what they will think. Don't you dare say anything about it! The second they hear about this dream, people will put labels on you, and believe me–they will not be nice ones."

As I write this out, it really seems so obvious now; this section is on spiritual warfare, correct? It seems appropriate that, even as I sit here in this hotel room, I am currently engaging in this unseen struggle. I am starting to get excited that the devil is afraid of this dream. Okay, I am ready....

This story came after an intense day. I was in a town four hours away taking my kids to a dental appointment. The temperature and winds outside were below zero. Little things kept going wrong and after an incredibly long day, due to the weather, we were forced to spend a second night in a hotel. I just wanted to be home. I was exhausted and I fell into a very deep sleep. Before I tell you more, I really need to pray first. Dear Heavenly Father, be with us as we walk through this dream together. Do not allow the enemy to instill fear. Reveal to us your truth and your divine power and authority through this story. We ask all these things in the name of your precious son, Jesus.

The Dream

Standing in a hallway, I see my 3-year-old playing with an adorable, demon-possessed toy. Because it appears harmless, I allow it to remain in my home. All of a sudden, the demon leaves the doll and enters my child. My initial indifference towards the toy turns to panic. I don't want this evil thing to respond in a way that would hurt my little girl, so I began to *negotiate* with it. A flash of hope: I recalled the story of Jesus casting a legion of demons out of someone and into a bunch of pigs.[15] I spoke to the demon and promised that if it didn't hurt my baby, I wouldn't send it to hell. The demon nodded and I used the name of Jesus to call it out.

I pulled a long, black, see-through scarf from my daughter's mouth and wrapped it around my arm. The scarf represented the demon. I stepped outside and walked into the street. The neighbors' Doberman stood at the end of their driveway, held back by a thick metal chain. Like in the bible story, I had found an animal to which I could send the demon, so I cast it into the dog.

The demon caused the Doberman to grow in size and strength. His chains snapped and released from his body. Growling, back arched, he moved towards me. The Doberman sprung up, running at me; I hugged my body, bracing myself for the attack. The dog stopped mere inches from me. I could feel his hot breath on my skin. The growling animal then transformed into a man. The man was an attractive, yet horrifying mix of previous boyfriends. His sickly-sweet words cause me to fall to my knees, cowering before him. I immediately feel ashamed, vulnerable, and humiliated. He towers victorious above me. With a thick demeaning tone, he remarks, "Oh, this is all that was needed to defeat you? I should have started out looking and speaking to you like this. I know exactly how you like to be treated."

Inside my mind, I want to fight! I know my only hope is to say Jesus' name, but I can't. I mumble disjointed words, saying, "No, I don't want that. Stop...please...stop. Go away."

In the presence of this demon, I feel the full weight of abuse. My thoughts cry out in desperation, "Jesus, open my mouth! Please help me say your name." I exhale trapped air as I am finally able to say Jesus' name. The demon takes a step back. I stand and take a good look at my opponent. I see the terror in his eyes. I realize, for the first time, his real fear of Christ in me. I point my finger in the demon's face and order, "Shut your mouth!"

The demon tries to speak, he holds his throat, he is really scared now. He is defeated and he knows it...I know it. I smile and say, "Go to hell." He disappears and I wake up to the sound of me whispering prayers in my sleep. I can hear myself praying protection over myself and my family. I realized that throughout the dream the Holy Spirit was praying on my behalf.

GOD HAS GOOD PLANS FOR ME AND MY FAMILY. SATAN HAS PLANS FOR MY FAMILY TOO. WHOSE PLANS DO YOU WANT?

This dream taught me some powerful lessons. My lack of concern over my child playing with the demon doll represented a very real threat in my home. I sometimes allow my children to engage in things that seem harmless, certain questionable TV shows and unsupervised freedom to search the internet. Deep down I know the cause of their unwillingness to share, mean words, or feelings of emptiness. Really, my children long for real things and experiences. Intentionality. They long for their mom to teach them good Christ centered things, to pray over them, play actual real life games and enjoy being in their presence. I want my children to learn to love and understand God's voice! The main reason parenting tires me is the constant battling of having to deal with the effects of my lazy parenting. God has good plans for me and my family. satan has plans for my family too. Whose plans do I want? Whose plans do you want?

The second lesson I learned came from sending the demon across the street into the neighbor's dog. Sometimes, when I fight the enemy or experience a trial...I only keep the enemy at bay. I chase the enemy from my home, but I don't change. I believe that no matter what, it will just come back. But I need to be actively battling, not passively. Never negotiate with the devil–remember, he is a liar. The joy of the Lord is where we find our strength, not fear.

Finally, standing no longer afraid is my favorite part of the dream. The enemy goes by another name–the accuser. He brings up our past sins, insecurities, and fears. He loves to tower over us, making us feel as though we are powerless to stop him. The truth is we bear the name of our Lord Jesus Christ, which when spoken shuts the mouth of our accuser. The devil trembles at the name of Jesus and is forced to leave. He has no power over us. He is a defeated foe.

God has used this dream in powerful ways to teach me some very important lessons on spiritual warfare. Here is the list...

1. Do not negotiate with the devil.
2. Do not lend the devil your ear. Nothing he says to you is worth listening to.
3. The instant the devil appears, speak truth. Speak aloud the name of Jesus; use scripture to remove any lies the enemy tells you. You must not allow those lies to take up residence within you.

4. Tell the devil to "shut his mouth" and send him directly to hell where he belongs!
5. Remove anything in your life you know is a door to the enemy. Sin and entertaining lies are an invitation for him to enter your home.

"You, however, are not in the flesh but in the Spirit, if in fact the Spirit of God dwells in you...For you did not receive the spirit of slavery to fall back into fear, but you have received the Spirit of adoption as sons, by whom we cry, "Abba! Father!"...Who shall separate us from the love of Christ? Shall tribulation, or distress, or persecution, or famine, or nakedness, or danger, or sword?...No, in all these things we are more than conquerors through him who loved us."

Romans 8:9, 15, 35, 37 (ESV)

"In the same way, the Spirit helps us in our weakness. For we do not know how we ought to pray, but the Spirit Himself intercedes for us with groans too deep for words. And He who searches our hearts knows the mind of the Spirit, because the Spirit intercedes for the saints according to the will of God."

Romans 8:26-27 (ESV)

Ephesians 6:10-13 was mentioned at the beginning of this chapter. Please take some time to allow these verses to sink in... even take it a few steps further and open your Bible to read more about putting on the full armor of God. Read these verses aloud as a prayer over your life, your children's life, your spouse's life. (This is how we weaponize scripture!) These verses, paired with this dream, brought to me a deeper level of forgiveness for my abuser and a clearer lens through which to view the world. I now see how all the abuse I experienced was not from my past boyfriends, but ultimately, orchestrated by the devil. When I hear the devil speaking to me, I need to not blame the person he is using as his mouthpiece. Rather, I must put the blame exactly where it belongs–with my accuser. Remember, Jesus did this with Peter when he declared, "Get thee behind me, satan!".[16]

It is not against flesh and blood that we are fighting. I have seen this in the life of my daughter, Lydia, who was adopted through Foster Care. Some very specific lies were spoken over her while she resided in her old home–The Enemy whispers, "No one wants you, you're a monster, there is something wrong with you, and you will always be alone. These words seem to appear at random times, even once during a church program she attended. A boy her age followed behind her, saying, "No one likes you. You will always be alone. There is something wrong with you." Relentless in his pursuit, the boy stayed committed to speaking these hurtful lies over her. He sat next to her in class, during game time he ran behind her, he followed her the whole night. How did this child know the exact lies to speak over my daughter? The truth is, he had no idea. This has happened to Lydia more than a few times in various situations and locations. She needed tools to fight; so, I reminded her–"over and over throughout your life satan is going to send people to say these specific lies over you. Lydia, you are a princess, cherished, loved, and never alone. You and Jesus have such a beautiful special relationship. You are precious to him. The devil sees the Holy Spirit in you; and it terrifies him. Your story is a threat to him. " She needed spiritual weapons for a spiritual problem. I wanted my daughter to be protected. These are her battle words: "When you hear 'you are broken', 'that you will always be alone', you say to the devil, "I am never alone; Jesus is always with me. Jesus has healed me. I am His Princess."

We need to know how to fight! We need to teach our children how to fight! We need to stand in the gap for our brothers and sisters in Christ and fight alongside them. Passivity is for losers! We need to be actively, passionately engaged in this battle. We must care about the things that matter to God. We need to get off our lazy butts and enlist. If you have been taking the back seat in your Christian faith, it is time to move into the driver's seat! These stories reveal the true danger of passivity with the devil. Do not be afraid of him. He is afraid of you, so put the fear right where it belongs!

I want to end my portion of this chapter with my all-time favorite quote from Martin Luther.

> *"Why should you fear? Why should you be afraid? Do you not know that the prince of this world has been judged? He is no lord, no prince any more. You have a different, a stronger Lord, Christ, who has overcome and bound him. Therefore let the prince and god of this world look sour, bare his teeth, make a great noise, threaten, and act in an unmannerly way; he can do no more than a bad dog on a chain, which may bark, run here and there, and tear at the chain. But because it is tied and you avoid it, it cannot bite you. So the devil acts toward every Christian."*[17]

Group Discussion Questions/Action Step/ Personal Reflection/Journal:

- In this chapter we discussed certain truths about who we are truly waging war against (2 Corinthians 10:3, Ephesians 6:12). Our battles are not against people! Who in your life are you experiencing conflict with? (A family member, friend, or coworker?) How should you manage this conflict (wage war) according to the Bible?

- John explains that we are from God and have overcome "them" in 1 John. Read 1 John 4:1-6 and write down who or what this verse means by the word "them." What do you notice in your own life that still needs to be overcome?

- The Bible uses some variation of the phrase "Do not fear" 365 times. Why do you think God reiterates this sentiment over and over to His people–to us?

Assignment: What are you currently fearing? Create a plan of action to confront and remove fear from your life!

Prayer

Dear Jesus, thank You for defeating the devil through Your death and resurrection. Through salvation, I am a new creation in Christ Jesus, and I have been granted the authority to defeat the enemy. Holy Spirit, reveal to me areas in my life where the devil has been lying to me. (listen)

In the name of Jesus, I cancel all the satan's authority over me in this memory/lie. All tormenting spirit assigned to me in this memory, I command you to go now in Jesus name. Holy Spirit, heal my heart and reveal Your truth about this memory.

In Jesus' name, amen.

If you've been dealing with fear, say this prayer:

By the blood of Jesus, I command the spirit of fear to go now. I have been given power and love and self-control by God and declare that you have no more rights in my life. Go! Holy Spirit, I receive your joy now, for You say in Your Word that the joy of the Lord is my strength.

In Jesus name, amen.

10–PASSIVITY IS FOR LOSERS

"A coward dies a thousand times before his death, but the valiant taste of death but once. It seems to me most strange that men should fear, seeing that death, a necessary end, will come when it will come."
William Shakespeare

"The real man smiles in trouble, gathers strength from distress, and grows brave by reflection."
Thomas Paine

Johnson

We, as Christians, are not called to passivity. We are called to an active, bold faith in Christ. A passive warrior would not last long on a battlefield. I am not talking about using worldly weapons, but our God given spiritual ones. By sharing my last dream, I am becoming less worried about what other people think and more excited to be open. On that note, I have another dream to share with you...

I stood in the road; my smaller children huddled around me for protection. Fire was coming up over the hill and large patches of brush were burning on either side of us. Embers of red and black ash fell from the sky. In my hands, I am holding an umbrella. I know God has given me this umbrella and He wants me to take my children one at a time through the fire. These instructions cause me to respond with confusion and worry. The full raging fire threatens, its flickering light flashing just behind the hill. I worry. I question, "What good will this umbrella do against fire? Which child should I take first?" I know I should trust God, but I don't know if we will survive the flames.

I woke up from this dream and immediately called Jenn. It was a blessing to immediately verbally process with my battle buddy. As we talked, I felt very connected to the feelings and concerns I had in the dream. Let me explain why. Do you remember the lie which was spoken over me by the enemy I wrote about in chapter 5? Let's go back over it again quickly.

"You are broken, you are too tired to fight anymore, give up. What good has giving everything done? It has destroyed you. You are alone. You will never have peace. I know how to hurt you, and more is coming. You are not strong enough to fight anymore, you cannot even get out of bed this morning! Your children are dying, and you cannot help them. You will watch your house burn before your eyes."

Fire. Satan used fire as a threat. An out-of-control forest fire for me was a good metaphor for what was happening in my life. I felt surrounded. It seemed as though I was in constant danger and unprotected. Satan is an abuser. He wants us to feel as though he has the power to do whatever he wants and there is nothing we can do to stop him. Helpless. The reality is we are by no means helpless or alone.

> *"I lift my eyes toward the mountains. Where will my help come from? My help comes from the Lord, the Maker of heaven and earth. He will not allow your foot to slip; your Protector will not slumber. Indeed, the Protector of Israel does not slumber or sleep. The Lord protects you; The Lord is a shelter at your right side. The sun will not strike you by day or the moon by night. The Lord will protect you from all harm; he will protect your life. The Lord will protect your comings and your goings both now and forever."*
>
> Psalm 121 (NIV)

I love this chapter in the Bible so incredibly much. It reminds me of the truth–I am not alone! Who is the One who is always with me? My Protector, my Heavenly Father, my Shelter, the one who keeps my feet from slipping. This is why we do not fear, because we know the One whom the wind and the waves obey. The One who stands in the fire with us and protects even our clothes from the smell of smoke. To bring this point home, I want to talk about one of my all-time favorite stories of fearlessness in the Bible–the story of Shadrach, Meshach, and Abednego. Let's take a moment to read two highlights from their story, which can be found in the book of Daniel.

> "Then Nebuchadnezzar in rage and anger gave orders to bring Shadrach, Meshach and Abed-nego; then these men

> were brought before the king. Nebuchadnezzar responded and said to them, "Is it true, Shadrach, Meshach and Abed-nego, that you do not serve my gods or worship the golden image that I have set up? Now if you are ready, at the moment you hear the sound of the horn, flute, lyre, trigon, psaltery and bagpipe and all kinds of music, to fall down and worship the image that I have made, *very well*. But if you do not worship, you will immediately be cast into the midst of a furnace of blazing fire; and what god is there who can deliver you out of my hands?"

Shadrach, Meshach and Abed-nego replied to the king, "O Nebuchadnezzar, we do not need to give you an answer concerning this matter. If it be *so*, our God whom we serve is able to deliver us from the furnace of blazing fire; and He will deliver us out of your hand, O king. But *even* if *He does* not, let it be known to you, O king, that we are not going to serve your gods or worship the golden image that you have set up." (Daniel 3:13-18)

These words the King used, "... and what god is there who can deliver you out of my hands?", are the words of an abuser. Basically, he is saying he can do whatever he wants to them and no one, not even their God, can save them. The response from these three young men being threatened with execution is powerful, fearless, and bold. They are willing to walk with God into and through the fire. They know He is big enough to save them. These men would rather walk into a furnace with God than turn away from Him.

Their bold faith led them to be thrown into a crazy hot furnace. The fire was so hot, it killed the guards who threw them in. So, what happened to these brave men? Did they burn up? Nope. When they entered the flames, they discovered they were not alone. Someone was already in the fire waiting for them. This person, most scholars believe, was Jesus. When the King looked into the flames, he said the mysterious fourth man looked like the son of God. This brings tears to my eyes. Instead of death, they were given a gift, one far greater than they could have ever imagined.

After being called out from the fire, these men were carefully examined. Let's take a moment and read about it.

> *"And the princes, governors, and captains, and the king's counsellors, being gathered together, saw these men, upon whose bodies the fire had no power, nor was a hair of their head singed, neither were their coats changed, nor the smell of fire had passed on them."*
>
> Daniel 3:27 (KJV)

THE FIRE HAD NO POWER OVER THESE MEN BECAUSE OF WHO WAS STANDING WITH THEM.

The fire had no power over these men because of who was standing with them. God knows the fire that rages in our lives. He is the only one who can give us the courage and ability to walk through our fires unsinged. God gives us umbrellas.

Sorbe and I sat with a dear friend of ours named Joe. We were engaging in a lovely Jesus-centered conversation, when Sorbe randomly brought up my fire dream. Honestly, it took me a second to remember what she was talking about. It had been a long time since I had that dream. Looking back now, when I first processed the dream with Sorbe I hadn't really thought very deeply about it. The umbrella part of the story made no sense to me, so I simply chose to ignore it and move on. I had initially thought the purpose of the dream was simply God letting me know He understood how I felt. As I listened to Sorbe recount the dream to our friend, it allowed me to take a step back and think. The point she was trying to make was that sometimes when we are following God, He will tell us to do something that doesn't make sense, like giving us an umbrella. When she had finished the story, Joe looked at me, puzzled, and asked, "Why did God give you the umbrella?" As soon as the question hit my ears, all the pieces came together. I got chills. Another question had come to my mind. *Why would someone give you an umbrella?* For the rain. God was not giving me an umbrella to protect me from the fire, but from the rain! This brings us back to Psalm 121:2-3: "My help comes from the Lord, the Maker of heaven and earth. He will not allow your foot to slip; your Protector will not slumber" (CSB).

We do not need to fear, because our Protector does not slumber. We serve a God who has the power to send the rain and who covers our heads to keep us dry. His love for us is complete. He doesn't give us meaningless tasks–everything is done for a purpose. The enemy wants us to focus on the fire, while Jesus wants us to focus on Him. We are not fearless because we personally are strong, but because we are loved by the One who *is*. Philippians 4:12-13 says, "I know how to be brought low, and I know how to abound. In any and every circumstance, I have learned the secret of facing plenty and hunger, abundance and need. I can do all things through him who strengthens me" (ESV).

I want to make something clear; I am not saying trouble will never come; the Bible states that in this world we will have troubles. What we need to understand is that God is equipping us to even face death. My daughter, Zoey, has taught me many lessons concerning this topic. One day she came up to me and asked, "Mom, why does everyone want to die in their sleep?" I answered, "I suppose it is because people are afraid of pain. The thought of dying is scary to them, and they don't want to think about it. Sleep is familiar and comfortable."

"HMM...WELL I WOULDN'T WANT TO DIE THAT WAY. I WOULD WANT TO DIE SAVING SOMEONE ELSE'S LIFE."

Zoey shrugged her shoulders, "Hmm...well I wouldn't want to die that way." This statement grabbed my full parental attention. Her simple statement confused me, piquing my curiosity. I wondered *what other way could someone possibly want to die?* I mentally made a list of all the ways a person could die...none of them seemed like a better option than sleep. Drowning? Car accident? Hypothermia? Heart Attack? Puzzled, I asked my daughter how she would want to die. Her response was far deeper than I ever expected from an 11-year-old, "I would want to die saving someone else's life."

What are we living for? Are we wanting a life filled with purpose and meaning? A true, active, running-the-race kind of life, or are we currently living a life of comfortable avoidance? We are all going to die someday. Shadrach, Meshach, and Abednego lived an active, all-in kind of life. Their lack of fear and active faith earned them a very rare place in the Bible...they are not examples of living stupid. They are examples of courage, integrity, and faith. What story do we want? Shadrack, Meshack, and Abednego–fearless men of God; or Jonah–shown up by a worm? God can still use us either way, but what do you want your story to look like?

> *"Finally, be strong in the Lord and in his mighty power. Put on the full armor of God, so that you can take your stand against the devil's schemes. For our struggle is not against flesh and blood, but against the rulers, against the authorities, against the powers of this dark world and against the spiritual forces of evil in the heavenly realms.*

Therefore put on the full armor of God, so that when the day of evil comes, you may be able to stand your ground, and after you have done everything, to stand firm."

Ephesians 6:10-13 (NIV)

"They promise freedom, but they themselves are slaves of sin and corruption. For you are a slave to whatever controls you."

2 Peter 2:19 (NLT)

"For everyone who has been born of God overcomes the world. And this is the victory that has overcome the world—our faith."(ESV) "And who can win this battle against the world? Only those who believe that Jesus is the Son of God."

1 John 5:4-5 (NLT)

Sorbe

So now you've learned that we have a battle on our hands, and we cannot be passive about it or it will affect us negatively. As we consider Johnson's intense dream, many of us can likely relate to overlooking a danger or threat to us or our family. Believe me, it's not intentional. Not really. It's more that we have not yet been trained to see it for what it is. We mentioned Ephesians 6 in the previous chapter. I'd like you to circle all the "all's" in verse 18 below.

"Praying at all times in the Spirit, with all prayer and supplication. To that end, keep alert with all perseverance, making supplication for all the saints." (ESV)

The MSG translation states it so well...

"Be prepared. You're up against far more than you can handle on your own. Take all the help you can get, every weapon God has issued, so that when it's all over but the shouting, you'll still be on your feet. Truth, righteousness, peace, faith, and salvation are more than words. Learn how to apply them. You'll need them throughout your life. God's Word is an indispensable weapon. In the same way, prayer is essential in this ongoing warfare. Pray hard and long. Pray for your brothers and sisters. Keep your eyes open. Keep each other's spirits up so that no one falls behind or drops out."

Ephesians 6:13-18

These verses are very active. They describe the very opposite of a passive Christian life. We are told to pray earnestly, to persevere in staying alert and to pray for one another. Learning to do this does not come easily, it takes work. I have heard nothing worth having comes easy. But it doesn't have to suck either.

As we read throughout the New Testament, we see how to live this active faith out. We can be encouraged that only Jesus did it perfectly–His disciples were learning as they went along just like us. I'd like to take another story from the Bible to show how the enemy went after one of Jesus' disciples, what Jesus did about it, and how the above verse is applied.

Listen to this... In Luke 22:31-34, we read that satan demanded to *have* Peter so that he might "sift him like wheat." Satan wanted to 'shake' Peter's life violently in order to destroy him and his testimony. Had that violent shaking taken place and Peter lost his faith, it would've been a true tragedy. We know Peter had his ups and downs, but he was a good student and learned from each of his mistakes. Jesus even called him 'the Rock' upon which He would build his church; so, it is no wonder satan wanted to sift him like wheat.

> *"And I say also unto thee, that thou art Peter, and upon this rock I will build my church; and the gates of hell shall not prevail against it. And I will give unto thee the keys of the kingdom of heaven: and whatsoever thou shalt bind on earth shall be bound in heaven; and whatsoever thou shalt loose on earth shall be loosed in heaven"*
>
> Matthew 16:18-19 (KJV)

These powerful words Jesus is speaking over Peter's life are ultimately a word for us, too–if we choose to step in. Let's turn to Luke 22:31–"Simon, Simon, behold, satan demanded to have you, that he might sift you like wheat..." BUT, if we continue to verse 32, we read something small, yet oh-so-very powerful. In fact, the next verse could easily be overlooked. *"But I have prayed for you* that your faith may not fail." Pause here. Read that verse again. *"But I have prayed for you* that your faith may not fail." Jesus steps in on Peter's behalf and prays for him. This is called *intercession*. In prayer, intercession is an appeal to God on someone else's behalf. It takes us right back to what Ephesians 6:18 is asking of us!

Did you notice the "but" leading verse 32? I love these kinds of buts! I'll bet I could write a whole book on all the "But, God" moments in scripture, as well as in my own life. "But [Peter], I have prayed for you that you wouldn't lose faith no matter the trials you may face." What a shame it would have been had Jesus not interceded through prayer on his behalf. Because of Christ's protective action when adversity came, Peter would now walk through adversity strong in his faith. This is called active faith–a "do" verse–and it shows us what we are to *do* for each other. We pray for one another, that our faith would not fail in times of stress, hurt, or brokenness.

Has your life been shaken so violently you fell from the mission that you were on? This is the enemy. This is what he does. He lies, and his deception will bring you out of grace and into ruin. But it doesn't need to stay that way. Like Johnson's dream in Chapter 9 where she stood up to the devil in Jesus' name and cast him and all his evil plans out, you can stand up too! Remember, you are an overcomer, and greater is He who is in you than he who is in the world.[1] With God on our side, we cannot fail. Do not lose heart–take a step in.

PASSIVITY WILL NOT BRING VICTORY.
PASSIVITY IS FOR LOSERS.

Maybe you feel like one of the zombies walking around inside the church. You've lost your way. You've lost your faith. You feel dead-eyed. Well, God is in the business of taking something from glory to glory.[2] Be open and trust the process, right? You need active faith in order to keep putting one foot in front of the other. It requires action to step in to pray for your hurting friend. Johnson needed active faith and prayer cover from a friend. Some days it took a monumental effort for her to even get out of bed. This active faith involves us proclaiming God's truth over our lives and rebuking the lies we've heard from the enemy. Our active pursuit of God's truth to combat the lies of the enemy is so very important. Passivity will not bring victory. Passivity is for losers.

I have a Christian friend with deep wounds from actively engaging in sexual sin. When she received Jesus Christ as her Savior, she received freedom from guilt and shame except for one particular area in her life–the shame of her sexual past. Here is her story, written by her and shared with her permission.

> *"It was in my own personal study/prayer time. I was reading a book by Lisa Bevere, where she mentioned that*

we are whole in Christ. I started crying and telling God that I had never felt whole. The label of the word "whore" had always haunted me. I grew up being called a whore, starting at the age of 8 yrs old. As I became older, I started sleeping around and became very promiscuous. Many partners, in and outside of even my marriage. It was so bad that even the weekend I gave my life to Christ and totally surrendered, had started out with me coming home from yet another adulterous affair. I had truly become that awful name I began to hear at the tender, and oh so naive & trusting, age of 8 yrs old! I believed I was that whore. I became that whore.

The guilt of all of these relationships I had followed me for years, even after I knew Jesus had forgiven me!! It was the one thing that kept me in bondage to my past. The very thing that satan knew he could use against me and I would continually succumb to the negative thoughts and feelings of unworthiness!!

BUT THAT DAY IN MY PERSONAL QUIET TIME WAS DIFFERENT!! GOD HAD A PLAN TO FREE ME FROM THE SNARE OF THE DEVIL....PRAISE GOD!

As I began crying out to God, I kept saying "I just want to be whole, complete, cleansed completely like Your word says I am! I know I'm no longer that whore!! Please Lord, help me get this!!!"

While I was praying this, in RED letters I wrote the word "WHOLE!!!" in the paragraph I was reading in the book. I opened my eyes and looked down at the page and I saw the word WHORE. ALL OF A SUDDEN THE "R" BEGAN TO MOVE UPWARDS ON THE PAGE, AND JUST BELOW IT WAS THE LETTER "L". IT WAS MOVING UP THE PAGE, AS WELL. THE "L" STOPPED RIGHT WHERE THE "R" HAD BEEN IN THE WORD WHORE, AND I LITERALLY SAW FOR THE FIRST TIME,

WITH MY OWN EYES, THAT I HAD BECOME "W.H.O.L.E."!!!! I started shouting Hallelujah Lord, I am WHOLE because of You!! I am NO LONGER that other person! I have been redeemed by the Blood....from Whore to WHOLE!!!

As Lisa said in this book, "But there is One to whom we belong, One who can heal our brokenness and fulfill our need for intimacy. It is the Spirit of God who hovers and makes us once again whole." (Adamant by Lisa Bevere)

Oh my goodness, I get chills every time I hear Christi share her story. Over and over in Christi's mind, she would hear the word *whore* and she absolutely believed that she was. Though she was no longer living the way she did in the past, that label followed her thoughts everywhere she went. But God's Word spoke to her... "In Christ we are made whole."[3] The verse jumped off the page and spoke directly into that shameful part of her life. Praise God!

Why did God's Word work so miraculously for Christi? The Word of God is living and active, sharper than any two-edged sword, piercing right through that division between our soul and our spirit. This message is taught in Hebrews 4. The Word of God is the sword. It is a tool to defeat the enemy and align our soul with the mind of Christ–just like what happened to Christi and what set her free!!

"For the Word of God is living and active, sharper than any two-edged sword, piercing to the division of soul and of spirit, of joints and of marrow, and discerning the thoughts and intentions of the heart."

Hebrews 4:12 (ESV)

"Now that we know what we have–Jesus, this great High Priest with ready access to God–let's not let it slip through our fingers. We don't have a priest who is out of touch

> *with our reality. He's been through weakness and testing, experienced it all–all but the sin. So let's walk right up to Him and get what He is so ready to give. Take the mercy, accept the help."*
>
> Hebrews 4:14-16 (MSG)

Jesus says, "I will remember their sins and their lawless deeds no more".[4] Sometimes, we can get a nasty lie dealt with right away; and sometimes, we must persevere with Jesus by focusing intently on what He says about us. We must never give up the fight for our wholeness! Proclaim the truth over and over again until you receive your breakthrough.

Remember where Johnson laid out the lies she was hearing? We took each of those lies and brought God's truth in to conquer them. We have to do that with every deceitful thing! What lies are you believing right now that need to be replaced with God's truth? It can happen so easily that we might not even know that we've accepted it. Take a moment right now to consider this question. Now, ask God to show you what He says about that specific lie and discover scripture to back up His truth. Once you have His words, write them down. Write them on your arm, say it out loud, scream it out if you must; but claim God's truth over your life and don't stop until you get your breakthrough!

In the name of Jesus, bind, reject and cast out the evil lie that has been abusing you! This is where freedom is found–in Jesus. He died and rose three days later for this breakthrough! Through this act of rejecting the lie, God will change your negative habits, too! If you took this first step with us to destroy a lie, your life is about to change. The devil is losing his grip on you, all because you are *open* to God, *trusting the process*, and cultivating a life of action by *killing fear*!

The day we accepted Jesus as our savior, sin no longer had power over us because we became a NEW CREATION and the old passed away; we are no longer slaves to sin! "Therefore, if anyone is in Christ (saved), he is a new creation. The old has passed away; behold the new has come."[5] If we don't understand and believe that verse, we will stay in the deception in which satan wants us to live. God has a much bigger, beautiful, life-filled calling for you–if you are willing to put your armor on and fight back, stay active and kick passivity to the curb! And yell, "Passivity is for losers!"

Group Discussion Questions/Action Step/ Personal Reflection/Journal:

- What areas of your life are fear-based or give you the feeling of being out of control? Do you see how "cowering" to fear, like Johnson described in her Doberman dream earlier, allows the lie to own you? Try to begin to identify the lies and destroy them–binding and casting them out.

- Do you feel encouraged to be more vulnerable–to be more honest with yourself and others like our authors and like Christi? Ask yourself what is really going on when you feel attacked. How do you now feel about telling satan to get behind you?

- Which part of the armor of God, described in Ephesians, are you most in need of remembering and utilizing more actively in your life?

Assignment: Take a bold step of faith–talk to a stranger about Jesus! Pray for a stranger when the Lord leads you! Intercede in prayer on someone else's behalf.

Prayer

Dear Jesus,

Please help me to see and to face the things of which I'm most afraid with honest vulnerability. Allow me to remember that nothing is insurmountable to you and that your perfect love casts out all fear. Reveal the lies the enemy has spoken to and over me. Help me to partner with You in order to cast out those lies. Surround me with a spiritually healthy and safe community who speak the truth, encouraging me to put on your armor daily.

In Jesus' name, Amen!

11–DEATH BLOW TO FEAR-KNOW YOUR IDENTITY

"It is when I turn to Christ, when I give up myself to His personality, that I first begin to have a real personality of my own."
C.S Lewis

"Faith enabled Moses to choose God's will, for although he was raised as the son of Pharaoh's daughter, he refused to make that his identity."
Hebrews 11:24 (TPT)

Johnson

We absolutely want the benefits of no longer being afraid. In this chapter, we are going to discuss how knowing our identity is a valuable tool for conquering fear. Sorbe will start us off with a powerful example from the book of Judges. As you read through this chapter, keep this question in mind... Who does God say you are?

Sorbe

Gideon steps onto the biblical scene in the book of Judges, where we find him hiding out in a winepress threshing wheat. In safer times, he would typically be threshing in an open area with the help of cattle. However, Gideon lacks confidence. He is fearful of the Midianite enemy and chooses to remain hidden while he works.

A stranger arrives, and sitting on a nearby stone, begins a conversation. We read, in Judges 6:11, this stranger is an angel; though, Gideon does not recognize him as such. "The Lord is with you, O mighty man of valor," the angel declares. What a way to start. It is interesting to me how the angel uses the terms "mighty" and "valor" to describe Gideon, all whilst he hides out to accomplish his work. Gideon surely looks around and wonders if the man is speaking to someone else. He knows he is displaying neither might nor valor. Disregarding the angel's words, Gideon responds with a remark which reveals his discouraged and bitter mindset, "Please, my lord, if the Lord is with us, why then has all this happened to us? And where are all his wonderful deeds that our fathers recounted to us, saying, 'Did not the Lord bring us up from Egypt?' But now the Lord has forsaken us and given us into the hand of Midian."[1]

Gideon takes no responsibility for Israel's plight. However, Judges 6:1 reveals the truth of Israel's situation: "The people of Israel did what was evil in the sight of the Lord, and the Lord gave them into the hand of Midianites seven years." Choices come with consequences, good or bad, and the truth is Israel had turned their backs on God. They chose their path and, ultimately, the consequences that came with it. This angel of the Lord stays within his original message and replies, "Go in this strength that is yours. Save Israel from Midian. Haven't I just sent you?"[2] Confused and incredulous, Gideon responds, "Please, Lord, how can I save Israel? Behold, my clan is the weakest in Manasseh, and I am the least in my father's house."[3] No doubt all sorts of thoughts are racing through his head at this point, but the angel of the Lord replies confidently, "*But* I will be with you, and you shall strike the Midianites as one man."[4]

You'll find out that Gideon takes some convincing. I do, too, Gideon. I can relate. He asks for a sign, for proof the angel is who he claims. Gideon brings him food and the angel of the Lord tells Gideon to take the meat and the cakes and set them on the rock. He then tells Gideon to pour the broth over the food. The man tips his staff and touches the meat and cakes. Fire springs up from the rock, consumes the food and the angel suddenly disappears. Now, Gideon is convinced this is an angel. I would be, too.

GOD CALLS AND THEN HE GOES *WITH* US.

We begin seeing the Lord talking to him in order to either encourage, comfort, or to give direction. I love this. God calls and then He goes *with* us. Gideon listens and obeys his first big task: tearing down what has ultimately caused Israel to look evil in the sight of the Lord. God is making His name known through this seemingly rebellious act and is setting the stage for what's coming next. The people were livid when Gideon burned down his father's altars set up for worship to other gods. Because of this, Gideon is given a surname, Jerubbaal, which means "the enemy of Baal." This shows his contrasting position of following *The Big-G God* and not *a god* (aka Baal). Right focus. Check!

His next task is even bigger, so Gideon is going to ask for some more confirmation. He reminds God of what He said through the angel, "If you will save Israel, as you have said..."[5] Two specific signs he asks of God and two signs he gets. The Lord says ask and you will receive. I'm telling you; God is hearing your prayers just as He heard Gideon's.

The next part gets interesting. Gideon has brought in help to go up against a common enemy, yet it is still only one-sixth of the enemy's hoard. God tells his valiant warrior, "There's too many of you for me to give Midian over into your hands, lest Israel boast over me saying it was all them."[6] Little by little, the Lord has Gideon trim down the war party until there are only 300 of them remaining.

> *"That same night the Lord said to him, "Arise, go down against the camp, for I have given it into your hand. But if you are afraid, go down to the camp with Purah your servant. And you shall hear what they say, and afterward your hands shall be strengthened to go down against the camp."*
>
> Judges 7:9-11 (ESV)

Either Gideon was scared or he was curious. Regardless, he went down to the camp with his servant. God totally catered to humanness, without shaming, and gave Gideon an opportunity to bolster his confidence. God is so loving. I can just imagine the Lord, if he's anything like a good earthly dad, eagerly watching the cool scene he would see Gideon experience in that moment.

I should mention here the Bible tells us the Midianites are "like locusts in abundance, and their camels were without number as the sand that is on the seashore in abundance."[7] I cannot even fathom this image. And here is Gideon, coming with 300 guys because God said so. It is enough. If you don't have faith, this definitely looks very stupid.

Gideon gets to the camp and there is a man telling a dream to his comrade. As he tells the dream, Gideon listens as the comrade explains the dream; "This is no other than the sword of Gideon the son of Joash, a man of Israel; God has given into his hand Midian and all the camp."[8] Okay, do you guys remember that Gideon said he came from the least clan and was the least in his own family? Now these guys, as numerous as locusts, are saying he is going to be given the whole camp by God? Wow. When God calls us into something, He will do some really awesome things if we allow him to use us as His vessels. I wonder if Gideon is believing the *valiant warrior* name the angel gave him or if he is just in shock and awe. We know as soon as he overhears these guys, he worshiped God! Remember, they have been living in fear and abuse from these people for seven years and Gideon is realizing, at this moment, they are about to be freed! It would be very hard not to make some noise at this point and even do some "in your face" dance in front of these two men. But Gideon stayed the course and went back to camp.

> *"Arise, for the Lord has given the horde of Midian into your hand." And he divided the 300 men into three companies and put trumpets into the hands of all of them and empty jars, with torches inside the jars. And he said to them, "Look at me, and do likewise. When I come to the outskirts of the camp, do as I do. When I blow the trumpet, I and*

all who are with me, then blow the trumpets also on every side of all the camp and shout, 'For the Lord and for Gideon.'"

Judges 7:15b-18 (ESV)

Trumpets, jars with fire in them, and shouts. This is how God is going to bring victory for His people. God will receive the credit, because there is no way any man could claim this victory is because of his own abilities. Gideon and his 300 men do it God's way. At the sound, the Midianites cry out, completely terrified and confused. In their terror, the enemy turns on one another and those who were not killed, fled far away.

Their abusers receive a death blow because Gideon steps into his calling and new identity. It is no longer about him, but about God. It takes some convincing, but Gideon accepts the call, listens, and obeys. God does not call the qualified; He qualifies those He calls.

On September 22, 2019, I received a new identity similar to Gideon. I have to confess something to you all–I used to have a pretty decent fear of women. They intimidated me and so I took the stance that most weren't worth knowing anyway. I knew my fear was not good for me and, in many ways, it kept me from something I heard was valuable. Sure, I had a couple of female friends, and though I was an open book and a friendly face, I really didn't feel the need to press in. Spend time with me or don't, I really didn't care that much. Why was I like this? I don't really know. I never really had a best friend. I was the extra friend. At times, I would be the favorite or I would be the lesser. Growing up, I found that guys were easier to get along with because girls could be so cruel. When I look back at photos from my past, I don't see someone who should have had insecurities, but I had them. Girls were fine, but I wouldn't have hung my hat on their relationships.

I loved working with youth, though. They were my favorite. They were fun. They were definitely less scary than adult women with all their issues. In 2017, I heard in my Spirit that God wanted me to step away from youth ministry and into women's ministry. I thought, "God, if you want that then you're going to have to bring women to me, because they scare me."

Knowing the only way to deal with insecurities is to face them head on, I thought I would start by being a greeter at my church. You know the position, right? You hold the door open for people, smile, and welcome them inside. It. Was. Hard. You need to look happy and sure of yourself. You need to make good eye contact, so people feel seen. Ugh–it challenged me. On the days I was not a greeter, I would come to church late, so I didn't have to stand around awkwardly and talk to people. I was typically the first one to leave for this same reason. I loved God like crazy and church felt so good to me, but my fear of talking to people about whatever small talk just kept me running out of there. There were times I longed to stick around and have someone to talk to, but often I would just find myself heading for the door. My husband, though a very confident man, had no desire to stick around either. He was my scapegoat. I had no idea how I was going to step into some form of women's ministry. Seriously, God was going to have to swing the door wide open.

During one of the last youth groups I attended, we received a call that our worship leader was rushing to the hospital because something was not right with the babe inside her tummy. She was in her third trimester. We circled up and prayed as hard as we knew how. Sadly, she delivered a baby who would never know the outside world. It was a crushing blow to us all.

Two years later we would be praying for this family again. This time their blessed baby would be born alive but needing to be in the NICU. It was during this time that there was a baby shower scheduled and the whole church family was invited. You may be wondering why this story is significant to me. Well, it's not for the reasons you may think. I don't go to baby showers if I can help it. I don't go to wedding showers, graduations, birthday parties... unless I feel an obligation to do so. They are just so awkward to me, and it is no wonder that so many of them serve alcohol; I must not be the only one needing some form of courage to get through it. Any of you relating with me, here? The older I got, the deeper the fear grew. I hid it well, but I realized it was an issue. Like *come on Sorbe, get a grip already. You were in the military, for goodness' sake*. Listen, you guys. I know. It was time to get the heck over it already.

On September 22nd, I told myself that I would go to the baby shower. I would suck up my fears because this family deserved it–they mattered way more than my insecurities. I'm pretty sure I pooped 3 times before I even left the house. I'm sorry, but if you don't deal with fear like this, you need to know it jacks with your body, too! I know there are some of you who are totally tracking with me here. I walked in late. Many people were already there and I began an internal conversation with myself to keep my feet moving forward, and though I did not want coffee, I desperately needed something to hold in my hand. For those of you who don't struggle in social situations, holding something in your hand is like a safety blanket to those of us who need something to do, something to look at, or to attempt to appear chill. Silly I know. You guys, I am chuckling at myself as I relive that night. It's ridiculous how gripped I was by fear. From an outside perspective, I have since been told by those in attendance that not a soul would have known this gripping fear terrorizing me from within. With as much confidence as I could muster, I headed toward a table. I sort of knew a woman at that table whom I had been telling myself to get to know (not that I had done much about it), but I was sure they wouldn't have a seat for me. That's how it usually went. So, I braced myself for rejection as I said the cleverest thing I could think of, "Hey is this where all the cool people sit? You wouldn't have room for one more would you?"

I had been praying, pleading with God the whole walk over to the table. *Please Lord, let them have a spot for me. Don't let me have to awkwardly sit alone while they all see me but ignore that I'm there.* Man, do you see my loss of hope in women? But there was another thing at work within me–God. He says in His Word that we can do all things through Christ who gives us strength.[9] I knew He wanted to stretch me, and I needed to allow Him to do it. I was sick of having this fear steal relationships and opportunity from me, but I still did not know how to get out from under it.

Turns out, those women had a spot for me. And you know what else? They were awesome. In fact, the woman at the table I had been wanting to know is one of my closest battle buddies now, praise God! That night was only going to get better from there, but it would look a little ugly at first. I drove home in shock and awe at God's goodness. I could not wait to tell Johnson about it! She prays for me to have women encounters all the time. It used to drive me nuts. Now, I am grateful she was interceding for me behind the scenes.

Here's the interesting part. Obviously, the Lord had a plan all along for me because that very night Johnson asked me this question, "Jenn, who does God say you are?" I heard immediately who He says I am. It hit my Spirit so hard, I wept. At first, I would not tell Johnson what God had told me. It was too awesome! He couldn't think that of me, could He? It seemed too good to hear from God, the very thing I would have wished. Though Mark was still struggling with his brain injury and living in his dark basement, Jenny got her husband on the phone to talk to me. I was on my knees and snot-crying. What was going on with me? Guys, I seriously could not stop. Somehow, I knew God was doing something in me that was going to be big. Mark knew me. We worked together with youth for several years and he knew how to speak into my life. Whatever was said, I was finally ready to share what God spoke over me, what He thought of me, what He named me. I knew when I said it out loud, I was going to accept it. If God said it, then this time I was going to believe it and trust He was going to qualify me into my role.

When Johnson asked me who God says I am, I heard loud and clear, "Valiant Warrior." And that very night when I wiped my tears, stood up, and said, "I am a Valiant Warrior," my fear of women was removed. Poof–gone! The Lord replaced my fear with a heart for women that moves me into places of deep relationship and intercession with them and for them. I was freed the night I stepped into my God given identity. Who does God say you are?

Let's look at scripture. Who does Christ say you are? What are some lies you are believing? How are you seeing these perceptions or lies manifest in your own life? Fear increases reaction, which increases defensiveness. Fear keeps you from taking risks. It makes you quick to be angry, quick to run, or quick to fight. But, and it's a big but, if you know Truth, who you are in Christ...worldly wisdom will not faze you. It will not penetrate your holy armor. Christ's identity is a free gift. Anyone who is saved has Christ's identity, whether they walk in it or not. It is powerful. It is hopeful. It is beautiful. People see it in you and gravitate towards it. It does not resemble the world at all. The world may even call it stupid. The time has come to talk about your identity.

> *"If someone says something less about you than what Christ says about you, it's because they either can't see who you are or they lost track of their own identity."*
>
> Bob Hasley

> *"The word of the Lord came to me, saying, 'Before I formed you in the womb I knew you, before you were born I set you apart; I appointed you as a prophet to the nations.'*

'Alas, Sovereign Lord,' I said, 'I do not know how to speak; I am too young.'

But the Lord said to me, 'Do not say, 'I am too young.' You must go to everyone I send you to and say whatever I command you. Do not be afraid of them, for I am with you and will rescue you,' declares the Lord."

Jeremiah 1:4-8 (NIV)

"For we are his workmanship, created in Christ Jesus for good works, which God prepared beforehand, that we should walk in them."

Ephesians 2:10 (ESV)

"So God created man in His own image, in the image of God he created him; male and female he created them."

Genesis 1:27 (NIV)

We read in 1 Corinthians 2 about how we are to have a reliance upon the Holy Spirit. Paul says, in Christ we speak God's wisdom that has been revealed to us through God. Many people don't see it, but we who seek God do, because He unveils it to us through the Holy Spirit. The passage goes on to say that the Holy Spirit, who lives inside of each of us who are saved, searches diligently, even the depths of God far beyond human understanding. It sounds like a superpower to me! And who doesn't want superpowers? I certainly want them, and I believe you do, too. We may not always know the thoughts of God in our humanness, but the Holy Spirit does. Paul continues, "Now we have received, not the spirit of this world (the devil), but the Holy Spirit who is from God, so that we may know and understand the [wonderful] things freely given to us by God."[10] Did you catch that? "Freely given to us." We don't deserve it, but because Holy Spirit lives in us, we get all that God has to give! And finally, my favorite part of this chapter comes at the very end:

TAKE THAT SATAN. YOU HAVE NO POWER OVER ME.

"For who has known the mind and purposes of the Lord, so as to instruct Him? But we have the **mind of Christ**."[11] Boom. Take that satan. You have no power over me. I have the mind of Christ! This verse should be our prayer.

Say it out loud with conviction. Say it over and over until it settles in your heart, and you feel breakthrough. I urge you NOT to skip this part! To be free from the enemy's hold over you, you MUST claim who it is you belong to. You belong to Christ. The devil will tell you this is not important. He will say *this is silly* or *what difference do words make*? He will tell you to not say it out loud but speaking ushers in authority over the devil. You may even be afraid right now to speak. All the more reason to pray! Prayers that claim the promises of God over your life are absolutely powerful and it terrifies the demons who have a hold on you. Declaration prayers like the one below removes the power of satan to have a claim over your life. Demons cannot hear your thoughts. You must say them out loud. Choose active faith over passive faith right now. Just do it.

I am the daughter/son of the Most High God! He has adopted me and He chose me before the foundations of the earth. How great is His love for me; as far as the East is from the West is His abounding love for me. So much so that He died for me! I was born on purpose, with purpose, for a purpose and no devil can take that away from me unless I let him. I am a new creation in Christ Jesus and my old life is no longer valid. I renounce all attachments to my old self, old habits, and soul ties that are not in accordance with the will of God. I take them all captive to the obedience of Christ and allow His holy sacrifice on the cross to cover my sin–past, present, and future. I am perfect in His eyes in my Spirit and am being made perfect in my soul. God, do a good work in me! I am open to you. Change my heart, oh God; may it be like you. Devil I rebuke you, but to you, Lord, I say come in and have your way in me. In the mighty name of Jesus, Amen.

Johnson

The time has come for another example of living stupid from the Bible. The parable of the talents is a story found in Matthew 25:14-18. "For it will be like a man going on a journey, who called his servants and entrusted to them his property. To one he gave five talents, to another two, to another one, to each according to his ability. Then he went away. He who received five talents went at once and traded with them and he made five more. So also, he who had the two talents made two more. But he who had received the one talent went and dug in the ground and hid his master's money" (ESV).

FEAR CAN KEEP US FROM LIVING OUT OUR PURPOSE.

Why did this man bury his talent in a hole? We find the answer in verse 25, "So I was afraid and went off and hid your talent in the ground. See, you have what is yours." Can you imagine being an employee and having your boss come in and ask, "What have you done all day?" And your response is "Well, I put protective bubble wrap over everything. I sat here and didn't move for fear of doing something wrong. See it looks exactly the same as when you left except for the bubble wrap." In this parable told to us by Jesus, we are given this warning...fear can keep us from living out our purpose. The scared servant was motivated by his fear of failure, which ultimately kept him from doing anything! The story ends with him being fired and his talent being taken away and given to the man who had made the best use of his talents. God has blessed each and every one of us with at least one spiritual gift/ability. Sorbe shared about Gideon, who was afraid, emotionally paralyzed and hiding from the enemy. But when he fully submitted to God's title for him of Valiant Warrior, he received the strength to face that very same enemy. God loves to give His children names that represent who they are and who He is calling them to be. These titles, given to us by God, reveal our true identity. They are a piece of a much larger puzzle, helping us to discover and live out our individual callings. Our special God-given talents are meant to be used, not hidden. I think this quote from Charles Spurgeon really helps us process this idea further. "Since most persons have but one talent, they are most often found saying, 'I have so little ability; I will not do anything. If I had five talents, I might become distinguished. If I had two, I might be useful. But with only one, I need not attempt anything. I am a private person–a mother obscure, with my little family around me–what can I do?' It is often a strong temptation from satan to those who have but one talent to hide that one with impunity."

Well, as a writer it feels slightly embarrassing that I did not know what impunity means...so I looked it up. Impunity means, "Exemption from punishment or freedom from the injurious consequences to an action." With this definition in mind, we see another reason we do not use our gift: we think it doesn't really matter. That if we do nothing, "nothing bad" will happen to us. In the story of the talents, we see that by doing nothing, we can lose everything. I love the question, "What can I do?" Answer? With God...a whole heaping lot! A better question may be, "What *can't* we do with the Lord's help?" The Bible is clear on the fact that we can do all things through Christ.

I love having conversations with people and often enter into discussions concerning this idea of stepping out and living fully for Jesus. One situation many people struggle with is...when someone asks for prayer, praying right away instead of waiting for someone else to do it. Prayer is a big struggle for many Christians. Almost every dinner with people from church will reach this inevitably awkward moment. The internal unspoken questions come. "Who will pray for the food?" *Are we going to pray? No one else is saying anything about it. Should I say something? I hope no one asks me.* Then someone with a quiet voice says, "Who wants to pray for the meal?" Panicked faces, people start avoiding eye contact. Then the quiet-voiced person, who thought by asking the question they would get out of praying, lets out a frustrated sigh. "I guess I can do it." Sighs of relief from everyone else. *Phew...I did not have to do it.* If we as believers feel uncomfortable praying with other Christians, how can we expect to be comfortable praying or talking about Jesus with non-Christians? Here is a short list of excuses I regularly hear from people.

"I am just not good at praying out loud," said an emergency room doctor. She is one of the most relaxed people I know. Nothing fazes her–except praying out loud. Recently, we prayed together on the phone and guess what...she absolutely can and is amazing at praying! Now, nothing fazes her.

"I don't know how to pray." I understand that this is a real question–one that even the disciples asked. But if this is your reason, let me ask you this...if you don't know how to pray, do you think God could help you learn?

Or maybe you have said this. "Other people are so much better than I am at praying." You know who is the best at praying?

The Holy Spirit. He loves us and prays on our behalf; we are called in a similar fashion to follow His example by praying for others. This, like anything we do, takes practice.

I want to leave you with one final example–a ninth grade boy named Tony Comer. I stood in a decent-sized group of High School students. I was on a mission to get volunteers for the nursing home, and this was my speech. "What has God called you to do? Do you love music? Come sing at the nursing home. We have residents that are bedridden who ask for someone to come sing to them. Do you have a heart to serve people? Please come and help with Bingo. Do you feel God calling you to be a pastor? We have services three times a week–you can sign up to speak. You are not too young to do what God is calling you to do. Public school kids, you have opportunities at school for God to use you. What are you called to do at your school? Homeschoolers, you have time. How are you using it to do what God has asked you? Whatever God has called you to do, you can practice those things at the nursing home."

A ninth-grade boy raised his hand and said, "I want to be a pastor. I feel God calling me into the ministry." Tony's knowledge of his calling, at a young age, led him to a commitment of preaching at the nursing home every Wednesday. When the residents at the nursing home heard a ninth grader was coming to preach, people who would normally never come to church were excited to attend. They quickly adopted Tony as their pastor. After only a year of being there, he was asked by a family to do their mother's funeral. Tony spent his High School years faithfully preaching at the nursing home. At the age of 19, he graduated with a Bachelor's degree in pastoral ministry. During his time volunteering, we would often talk about a famous phrase in the book of Esther, "For such a time as this." This is in reference to a speech given by Mordecai to Queen Esther. This royal was scared to go before the king on behalf of her people, but her uncle knew the words to move Esther past her fear, and those words are found in Esther 4:14. "If you keep silent at this time, relief and deliverance will come to the Jewish people from another place, but you and your father's family will be destroyed. Who knows, perhaps you have come to this royal position for such a time as this." Much like Esther, Tony believed that God had called him to speak, "For such a time as this." What if Tony had been afraid? What if he said, "I am too young. Will my friends make fun of me? I am not ready."

Thankfully, he chose to not listen to fear, because being a pastor was exactly the very thing he had been created to do. Identity, knowing with confidence your purpose, trusting that Jesus knows what is best for you, is the place you want to be. Understanding your identity in Christ will be the final death blow to fear. Time to walk in freedom, no longer afraid!

Group Discussion Questions/Action Step/ Personal Reflection/Journal:

- What was your main take away from chapter 11?

- What fears are holding you back?

- What are your spiritual gifts? (If you do not know what your gift is, there are many free online Christian sponsored tests. Simply type “free spiritual gift inventory tests” into your favorite search engine.)

Assignment: Take some time this week to pray with someone and seek the Lord concerning your identity. Who is it that God says that you are?

Prayer:

Dear Jesus,

I confess that I have not been living in the fullness of this Christian life, but I want to be. Lord show me how. Lord, I confess that I have been blaming You for things that the devil has done to me. I'm sick of the devil's abuse so Lord, I ask You to open my spiritual eyes to see where I have allowed him a place in my life. I want to be free! Also, Lord, I know there are people, like me, who blamed You for things the devil did and thus couldn't accept You in their lives. Make me courageous Lord to share with them what I am learning. I rebuke all fear in Jesus' name and I put on the full armor of God right now. I have the mind of Christ and I can do all things through You who gives me the strength to do them!

In Jesus' name, Amen!

NO LONGER STUPID

Anyone has the ability to experience this supernatural love. I do know; however, it requires some chasing after the heart of the Father. Seek Him, talk to Him in prayer, read books about Him, talk to your battle buddies about Him... live Him and breathe Him constantly.

Sorbe

"Or are you ignorant of the fact that all of us who have been baptized into Christ Jesus were baptized into His death? We have therefore been buried with Him through baptism into death, so that just as Christ was raised from the dead through the glory and power of the Father, we too might walk habitually in newness of life [abandoning our old ways]. For if we have become one with Him [permanently united] in the likeness of His death, we will also certainly be [one with Him and share fully] in the likeness of His resurrection. We know that our old]self [our human nature without the Holy Spirit] was nailed to the cross with Him, in order that our body of sin might be done away with, so that we would no longer be slaves to sin. For the person who has died [with Christ] has been freed from [the power of] sin.

Romans 6:3-7 (AMP)

Antonyms for STUPID:

Bright, careful, intelligent, prudent, reasonable, sensible, serious, sharp, smart, thoughtful, wise, cognizant, and responsible."

Roget's 21st Century Thesaurus, Third Edition Copyright © 2013 by the Philip Lief Group.

12–REMEMBER THIS

Remember: intransitive verb

1. To recall to the mind with effort; think of again.
2. To have (something) arise in one's memory; become aware of (something) suddenly or spontaneously.
3. To retain in the memory.

The American Heritage® Dictionary of the English Language, 5th Edition.

Johnson

Prepare yourself for this next chapter; if taken to heart, it will obliterate your desire for worldly, empty life-sucking things. It will provide you with the key for radical change. Sorbe and I added this chapter after we thought the book was finished. We have personally experienced how powerful the love of God is and we want you to realize it too. Once you experience His tremendous love, nothing in this world compares. Addicts hand over their crack pipes for it. Millionaires walk away from their fortunes because of it. People choose God over their careers, their families, their very lives. My daughter Caelyn just snuggled in next to me on the couch and asked, "Mom, what are you writing?" As I shared with her what I wrote, she gave me her definition of God's love.

> *"God's love: It is happiness that you've never experienced before. It feels super nice. Lovely. It is like you are in heaven. Your heart feels like it is going to explode! After you experience God's love you see things that you have never seen before. You want to be nice to everyone and you can't help but love them."*
>
> Caelyn- age 8

God is truly amazing! Children can teach us so much if we take time to listen. Adults tend to overcomplicate things that we understood in simplicity as children–concepts like love.

Sorbe

The Bible has some powerful things to say about our kids, too.

"Oh Lord, our Lord, your majestic name fills the earth! Your glory is higher than the heavens. You have taught children and infants to tell of your strength, silencing your enemies and all who oppose you."

Psalm 8:1-2 (NLT)

"Don't you see that children are God's best gift? The fruit of the womb his generous legacy? Like a warrior's fistful of arrows are the children of a vigorous youth. Oh, how blessed are you parents, with your quivers full of children! Your enemies don't stand a chance against you; you'll sweep them right off your doorstep."

Psalm 127:3-5 (MSG)

What is love? Its' definition is under attack today. Different views of what love is come at us from all angles. It can be confusing and overwhelming. Do we have to pick a side? Do we have to hold a sign? Walking this intentional road with Johnson has given me a glimpse of a love I have never felt previously. It is supernatural. It is pure. It is heavenly. It is hard for me to explain but I will do my best because I want you to experience its power. Once you have, you will never want any counterfeit. Honestly, it's a love worth dying for.

Johnson brought up Shadrach, Meshach, and Abednego in an earlier chapter as an example of *No Fear*, but do you know why they were able to face such a fate with boldness and resolution? Because they had to have known the love of the Father God in a supernatural way that went deeper than their fears. I have felt this. Look, no one is threatening me with physical death like these men. There is, however, a stirring in my Spirit and my soul that is causing my natural selfishness to melt away. I am seeing people differently. I care emphatically. I actually care about humans on a level that I have never known possible. It will hit me out of the blue. I can be sitting in a restaurant and my heart bursts with love for the people around me, nearly bringing me to tears as I survey the room. In those moments, I feel God's love for others. They aren't doing anything to deserve it, yet He loves them so, so much. I am blown away by it and it's changing me.

What makes me so special to experience this you may ask? Nothing, necessarily. Anyone has the ability to experience this supernatural love. I do know; however, it requires some chasing after the heart of the Father. Seek Him, talk to Him in prayer, read books about Him, talk to your battle buddies about Him... live Him and breathe Him constantly. It's not a head thing, though our thought life does come into play. The thought process needs to be there, but it's so much more. It's deeper. It's a longing for more in our born-again life. I don't want to live a boring Christian existence or, even worse, a finger-pointing Christian lifestyle. I want to embrace how Jesus lived His life, loved others, and stood for truth. If you've made it this far through this book, my guess is this is your desire, too.

[THE DEVIL] DOES NOT WANT YOU TO FEEL GOD'S LOVE, AND IT TERRIFIES HIM WHEN YOU DO. GOOD. HE NEEDS TO BE SCARED.

Jesus flipped tables when he saw God's house on earth being disrespected. He loved people who were hated, despised, judged, and He openly spoke to them about God's love for them. He stood in the face of religiosity that had lost its grace for people. He took time daily to pray to God the Father. He allowed the Holy Spirit to flow through Him and He used it to bring life, healing, and deliverance to seekers. He sought the Father's will and obeyed it. He denied himself with true submission to a purpose driving His life on earth. You have purpose, too. So do I. Your purpose is valuable. You are valuable. I hope you know that you are worth more to God than you may ever have the ability to comprehend. The devil doesn't want you to know this. He does NOT want you to feel God's love, and it terrifies him when you do. Good. He needs to be scared.

> *"Now the scribes and Pharisees brought a woman who had been caught in adultery. They made her stand in the center of the court, and they said to Him, "Teacher, this woman has been caught in the very act of adultery. Now in the Law Moses commanded us to stone such women [to death]. So what do You say [to do with her—what is Your sentence]?" They said this to test Him, hoping that they would have grounds for accusing Him. But Jesus stooped down and began writing on the ground with His finger. However, when they persisted in questioning Him, He straightened up and said, "He who is without [any] sin among you, let him be the first to throw a stone at her." Then He stooped down again and started writing on the ground. They listened [to His reply], and they began to go out one by one, starting with the oldest ones, until He was left alone, with the woman [standing there before Him] in the center of the court. Straightening up, Jesus said to her, "Woman, where are they? Did no one condemn you?" She answered, "No one, Lord!" And Jesus said, "I do not condemn you either. Go. From now on sin no more."*
>
> John 8:3-11 (AMP)

The passage you just read, like all others in the Bible, is there intentionally. It is there for us to not just read, but truly absorb. This woman was caught in the act of adultery when those men grabbed her and pushed her in front of Jesus to condemn her. Can you imagine the humiliation that poor woman felt at that moment? I cannot even imagine, but I'll bet some of you reading this absolutely can. My heart goes out to you as I write this. I feel my heart being squeezed and I tearfully pray for you and the pain you have endured. This was written FOR YOU. Please read it again. Don't move on. This book is written on purpose and with purpose, for you. No, devil, you cannot have this moment. I deny you access to this reader's deliverance in the name of Jesus. You will not deny them access to Christ's forgiveness and healing. You've done enough to them, and you cannot have them any longer, in Jesus' name. Amen.

Jesus did not add to her humiliation. He refused to shame her. He made them consider their own sin and they had to walk away. They were in no position to accuse her. Christ's love and acceptance came without requirement. She was welcome to it as she was. It was open to those accusers, too, if they wanted it.

> *"**Little children (believers, dear ones), you are of God and you belong to Him and have [already] overcome them [the agents of the antichrist]; because He who is in you is greater than he (satan) who is in the world [of sinful mankind].***
>
> *They [who teach twisted doctrine] are of the world and belong to it; therefore they speak from the [viewpoint of the] world [with its immoral freedom and baseless theories—demanding compliance with their opinions and ridiculing the values of the upright], and the [gullible one of the] world listens closely and pays attention to them...*
>
> *Beloved, let us [unselfishly] love and seek the best for one another, for love is from God; and everyone who loves*

[others] is born of God and knows God [through personal experience]. The one who does not love has not become acquainted with God [does not and never did know Him], ***for God is love. [He is the originator of love, and it is an enduring attribute of His nature.]***

By this the love of God was displayed in us, in that God has sent His [One and] only begotten Son [the One who is truly unique, the only One of His kind] into the world so that we might live through Him.

In this is love, not that we loved God, but that He loved us *and sent His Son to be the propitiation [that is, the atoning sacrifice, and the satisfying offering] for our sins [fulfilling God's requirement for justice against sin and placating His wrath]. Beloved, if God so loved us [in this incredible way], we also ought to love one another."*

1 John 4:4-5, 7-11 (AMP)

...not that we loved God, but He loved us. Please get this. It's not about you. It is and it isn't. He came to earth to love us and free us. That part is absolutely about us. But his loving us is not because we're doing something to receive it. He did it despite our sad state. It's all Him. The gravity of being loved so purely, so unconditionally is...well I don't even have words to truly capture it. None of our words touch what it is. I keep hearing the word, "otherworldly." It's out of this world. It's heavenly. It is a touch from heaven while we walk on this earth, and it changes us in all the best ways. Praise God.

Johnson

> *"In this [union and fellowship with Him], love is completed and perfected with us, so that we may have confidence in the day of judgment [with assurance and boldness to face Him]; because as He is, so are we in this world. There is no fear in love [dread does not exist]. But perfect (complete, full-grown) love drives out fear, because fear involves [the expectation of divine] punishment, so the one who is afraid [of God's judgment] is not perfected in love [has not grown into a sufficient understanding of God's love]. We love, because He first loved us."*
>
> 1 John 4:17-18 (AMP)

I had to add a few verses to Sorbe's 1 John 4. That whole chapter is just so incredible. "In this [union and fellowship with Him], love is completed *and* perfected with us." Wow! Such a powerful life changing verse! Letting Jesus love you can be a difficult concept for some of us Bible believing Christians, because it seems almost prideful. It is actually the opposite; letting Jesus wash your feet is humbling. Would you honestly feel totally comfortable with your Savior washing your feet? Or giving you an actual kiss on the cheek? What if He placed his hands on you to pray a blessing over you? Jesus loves you, and He has a Biblical reputation for getting in people's personal space to love them. He died for you. You will never be able to out-love Him. Never. God is the best at everything, including loving people. God is love. The way Jesus loves me, reveals how I am to love others. Remember: We are able to love because he first loved us.

GOD TRANSFORMED THE WORST SEASON OF MY LIFE INTO THE BEST.

God transformed the worst season of my life into the best. A while after Mark was brought out of the basement, he needed another knee surgery. What was supposed to be a day surgery turned into a weeklong hospital stay. I slept at the hospital on a cot next to my husband. I washed my clothes in the hospital bathroom because I didn't want to leave his side. God showed up in so many ways. I didn't always seek out help but help came. Earlier in the book, I said I didn't drink coffee. Well, I do now. A dear old friend from High School took me out for dinner and fancy caffeinated chocolate drinks. She offered to do my laundry for me...I said no because I felt guilty. I felt like she had already done so much for me. Later, another friend scolded me, "Jenny! Jesus is trying to take care of you, please let him do your laundry!"

GOD COMFORTED AND ENCOURAGED MY HUSBAND BY TURNING SOMETHING HARD TO TALK ABOUT INTO A POWERFUL STORY.

One difficult night Mark was not able to use the bathroom. He was embarrassed and struggling, but he felt led to pray for one of his students who was doing mission work in another country. Shortly after his prayer this very same student called him to check on him. Their team had gotten food poisoning and had all gotten sick. His vulnerability about his struggle allowed her to open up and they both prayed for each other. God comforted and encouraged my husband by turning something hard to talk about into a powerful story.

When we needed to leave the hospital, we were both still scared. Mark was not ready to leave. A random social worker who we had not talked to before, other than her giving us normal official hospital information, popped her head in our room to say, "Mark Johnson, God is not done with you!"

One of our favorite nurses, a sweet Ethiopian Christian, called our hospital room from her personal phone on her day off. I am crying right now as I write this. God is so good! She wanted to pray with me and read her favorite Bible verse. That call could have gotten her in trouble, but she was living out her faith in Christ. Out of love, she did what He had asked her to do.

God gave Sorbe a dream, bringing her into my life as a friend, prayer warrior, and now a ministry partner. There is nothing like the love of Christ. The world does not offer anything that compares. Without Jesus, this story would be a tragedy. I owe my very life to Christ. I could not have walked this road without Him, and neither can you. He knew exactly what I needed. He knows exactly what you need, as well. Moses was desperate to experience more of God. Desperate. Hungry. Longing. These things can only be satisfied through letting Jesus do everything for you. Don't do a single thing without him. Do your laundry with him, invite him to bake cookies with you, take him with you to soccer practice. That sweet nurse brought Jesus with her to her job, and now I am using her as an example in this book. She loved Jesus in a way that people could tell she was different. You can tell when someone really loves God and feels loved by Him. They shine because His love radiates from them. They are a light. This is how I want to live. This is how we, as believers, are meant to live.

Jesus tells us in Mark 12:30-31, "Love the Lord your God with all your heart and with all your soul and with all your mind and with all your strength.' The second is this: 'Love your neighbor as yourself.' There is no commandment greater than these."

WE LOVE BECAUSE [JESUS] FIRST LOVED US. HE WANTS YOU TO LET HIM LOVE YOU, SO YOU CAN LOVE OTHERS. IF YOU REMEMBER THIS ONE THING, YOU WILL BE UNSTOPPABLE.

There is no greater commandment than these and we love because He first loved us. I think we often over complicate the Christian message. It really is quite simple. Jesus wants to do your laundry, take away your sin, do everyday life with you. He wants you to let him love you, so you can love others. If you remember this one thing, you will be unstoppable.

Group Discussion Questions/Action Step/ Personal Reflection/Journal:

- What things does Jesus love about you?

- What is the meaning of your name?

- What area of your life do you need to experience God's grace, healing, or love?

Assignment: Spend time alone with Jesus. Play worship music. Talk to Him. Journal. Read your Bible. Talk to a friend. Let Him love you.

Prayer:

Dear Jesus,

Give me eyes to see a friend in need. I want to be used by You Lord. I love you so much. I'm open.

In Jesus' name, Amen!

13–READY FOR DEPLOYMENT

"Alexander, Caesar, Charlemagne, and I have founded empires. But on what did we rest the creations of our genius? Upon force. Jesus Christ founded his empire upon love; and at this hour millions of men would die for him."
Napoleon Bonaparte

"Beloved, I say, let your fears go, lest they make you faint hearted. Stop inspiring fear in those around you and now take your stand in faith. God has been good and He will continue to manifest His goodness. Let us approach these days expecting to see the goodness of the Lord manifest. Let us be strong and of good courage, for the Lord will fight for us if we stand in faith."
Francis Frangipane

Johnson

Are you ready? This is the very last chapter in the book. Sorbe and I have loved going on this journey with you. Our goal is to encourage, inspire, and cement in your brain this lifestyle of no longer doing things your way. We are praying that as you depart from this book, you will forever carry these powerful tools.

> *<u>Open</u>: Living a life that is fully surrendered and open to Jesus.*
>
> *<u>Trust the Process</u>: Faithfully following and trusting the Holy Spirit wherever He leads you.*
>
> *<u>No Fear</u>: Understanding who you are in Christ and boldly standing shoulder to shoulder with fellow believers completely unafraid and unashamed.*

What I am imagining right now are great speeches throughout history. Picture with me....a strong leader standing before their army on the eve of battle. Think of Joan of Arc, William Wallace depicted in the movie "Brave Heart", Winston Churchill, Abraham Lincoln, or even Robin Hood. You and I are standing together amongst a vast army, preparing to face our true enemy. I do not have the words to give you the strength to face what lies ahead, but the Bible does. Let's read Deuteronomy 20:1-4,

> ***"Laws of Warfare:*** *When you go out to war against your enemies and see horses, chariots, and an army larger than yours, do not be afraid of them; for the LORD your God, who brought you out of the land of Egypt, is with you. When you are about to go into battle, the priest is to come*

forward and address the army, saying to them, "Hear, O Israel, today you are going into battle with your enemies. Do not be fainthearted or afraid; do not be alarmed or terrified because of them. For the LORD your God goes with you to fight for you against your enemies, to give you the victory." (ESV)

No matter what lies ahead. God promises to be with you. God tells His people not to be fainthearted or afraid. Why are we not afraid? Because the same God who brought Israel out of Egypt is the same God who fights for you, not against you. This bold "all in" kind of faith inspires us. Leading us to desire more than a comfortable couch sitting existence. I wrote an allegorical fantasy novel entitled, The House of Envy. There is a quote from that book I would like to share with you. These words are how I picture what you and I are being called into "...Once you were a fish out of water, gasping for air. I placed you in a beautiful glass bowl filled with water; that is where you are now. You are breathing for the first time and are amazed by merely living. But my desire is for you to live in my will, which will open your eyes to a sea of joy and amazement. I never intended for you to be happy in a bowl, because I created you for the ocean."

God is calling us (the Church) out of our bowls and into the ocean. Are you ready? Excited?

Sorbe

It doesn't take much for me to visualize a war scene, to hear a commander's speech, to see men's faces preparing themselves for battle. They know it's a hard road ahead, but this is why they've trained. This is why you've trained.

Johnson

In my personal storm, God was with me. Without Him there would be no doughnut story, no spiritual warriors sent to fight alongside me, no miraculous healing from past relationships, no hope and no "Your Way Is Stupid" book. Everything good from this story came from Jesus. He is the reason Sorbe showed up as my battle buddy. The LORD answered my prayer for my husband and carried him out of that dark basement. God saw me struggling, trying my best to walk out my faith on my own. Doing life mostly my way, ultimately trying to carry my canoe in a feeble attempt to impress my Heavenly Father. My way was exhausting, stupid, and way more than I could handle. I needed a better way. I needed God to reveal himself in my story, a captain to steer my Titanic far away from an iceberg. In desperation, I cried out for help, and He gave me so much more than a rescue. He gave me an abundant life. This is the moment I wish I could reach out from this book and shake you, and say, "Really, please believe me! Your way is stupid! His way Is so much better!"

God took the darkest season of my life and transformed it into the brightest. Spiritual growth and passion that once came only from attending big Christian events or mission trips is now happening daily. Praying regularly with a friend is a vital part of this life. Do not underestimate the benefits of practicing being open, trusting the process, and no fear with others.

We would like to send you out with some final encouragement from you Heavenly Father...

> *"And let us consider how to stir up one another to love and good works, not neglecting to meet together, as is the habit of some, but encouraging one another, and all the more as you see the Day drawing near."*
>
> Hebrews 10:24-25 (ESV)

"Let the word of Christ dwell in you richly, teaching and admonishing one another in all wisdom, singing psalms and hymns and spiritual songs, with thankfulness in your hearts to God."

Colossians 3:16 (ESV)

"Again I say to you, if two of you agree on earth about anything they ask, it will be done for them by my Father in heaven. For where two or three are gathered in my name, there am I among them."

Matthew 18:19-20 (ESV)

Togetherness is important. Community is valuable. The people and relationships God has placed in your life are priceless and of eternal significance. They matter. Invest yourself fully into the plan God has for you. Stupid is not the place any of us want to stay. We must soak in and live every single thing God asks of us, because His way is so much better! Vastly better. Better than better. It is absolutely the best life. Step into the life you were created to live.

Johnson/Sorbe

This "stupid book" as we affectionately call it, is a conversation between friends and the Lord. We have loved this journey with you! We've laughed, cried, and learned so much through praying and discussing God's word together. Throughout this book our words have been separated in this conversation, but to close we feel led to send you out in true battle fashion–with a speech!

Go forth mighty warriors of the faith! You are equipped by the King of Kings to wage war against the powers of darkness. We are more than conquerors in Christ Jesus. Be of great courage, for you are amongst brothers and sisters in arms. You do not fight alone. Your King has gone before you in this battle. His perfect plan has given you assured victory over your adversary, the devil. Remember that satan is a defeated foe! May God give you the courage to boldly share the salvation message to all held captive by the enemy. You possess the only hope mankind has: the Gospel. Cast off all fear, be open to your Savior, trust Him, and put on the full armor of God. It is time for dry bones to come to life! The church has awakened from its zombie state. Arise; unsheathe your spiritual weapons. Warrior, this is your deployment!

Remember; be open, trust the process, and have no fear!

Hello Friends!

To all of you that read Your Way is Stupid, THANK YOU! We would love to hear from you. Your input is very important to us and we value what you have to say. Many of you have shared during open discussion at your gatherings and no doubt it has brought you closer to one another. Sharing really is caring. We would like to ask for your feedback that we can use in the promotion of our book moving forward. Below, we have listed some thought-provoking questions and we would enjoy hearing your thoughts regarding them. But don't let our questions limit you. Please feel free to share anything else you would like to add.

What has God done or shown you as you have read this book?

Have you learned anything new?

What stories stood out to you and why?

Were the Bible stories that we shared, presented to you in a new and unique way that you had not previously considered?

What made you laugh? What made you cry?

Did you do any of the assignments? We'd love to hear any of your testimonies.

Did you read the salvation part and make a commitment to accept Jesus into your life for the first time?

Did you find that you wanted to share parts of the book with others that may not be reading the book?

Would you please consider writing a review of Your Way is Stupid *right now? FYI–This will be a VERY powerful tool for us to get this message out to others. Even if you think you are no good with words, Jesus is! Trust Him to help you share what is on your heart regarding this book and the impact it made on your life.*

www.jenandjennministries.com
www.facebook.com/jenandjenn

Once again, thank you so very much for reading our book. We are excited to see what the Lord does in and through this book. May it bring Him all the glory! In Jesus' Name!

Sincerely Your Authors,
Jen Johnson & Jenn *Sorbe*

WEAPONIZED SCRIPTURE

(Ephesians 1:17-18, 19a)

A prayer for you...

We pray the God of our Lord Jesus Christ, Father of glory, may give you the Spirit of Wisdom and of Revelation in the knowledge of God, having the eyes of your hearts enlightened, that you may know what is the hope to which He has called you; what are the riches of his glorious inheritance in the Saints, and what is the immeasurable greatness of His power toward us who believe.

Your prayer...

Dear Lord, thank you for calling me to be a light in this world while I am here (Matthew 5:16). I pray that I will receive the Hope, which is in You Lord, to do what You ask of me. I am Open to You. Use me and mold me and protect me as I step fully into Your call and purpose over my life.

I know, Lord, that you have plans to prosper me and to give me hope. You hear my prayers (1 Peter 3:12). I Trust you. When I feel alone, I will seek you; because everyone who seeks you, finds you (Jeremiah 29:13).

Fill me with the knowledge of Your will, God, in all spiritual wisdom and understanding (Colossians 1:9) so that I may walk in a worthy manner of You and bear good fruit (Colossians 1:10).

Though my emotions sometimes make me think You're not there, I know You never leave me or turn Your back on me

(Deuteronomy 31:6). All my Fears, I give to you God (1 Peter 5:7). I take every thought captive to the obedience of your Son, Jesus Christ (2 Corinthians 10:5), so that no one can take me captive by philosophy and empty deceit (Colossians 2:8). I declare that I have the mind of Christ (1 Corinthians 2:16) and no weapon formed against me will prosper (Isaiah 54:17), in Jesus' name. I declare that I am being strengthened with all power according to Christ's might for all endurance and patience with joy. The joy of the Lord is my strength! You, Lord, have qualified me to share in the inheritance of the Saints in Light and You, God, have delivered me from the domain of darkness. You have transferred me into the kingdom of Your beloved Son, Jesus. In Jesus, I have the redemption and the forgiveness of sins (Colossians 1:9-13); and so, from a place of authority in heaven and by the covering of Jesus's blood over me, I rebuke all accusations the devil brings against me and my family. In Jesus' name, I declare I am clean, and that Jesus remembers my sins no more (Isaiah 43:25, Hebrews 10:14-18, Psalm 103:12, Romans 8:1, 1 Peter 5:8, James 4:7)!

Fill me with your Holy Spirit Lord because I desire it (Acts 2:4). I put on the whole armor of God, so I may stand against all the flaming arrows of the enemy. I put on the helmet of salvation and the breastplate of righteousness. I buckle the belt of Truth around my waist and put on the shoes that give me the readiness to keep my steps sure. I grab my shield of faith and my sword of the Spirit (Ephesians 6:10-17). I declare I will have joy in the Lord, for it is my strength (Nehemiah 8:10). In You Lord, I cannot fail. I can do all things in Christ, who gives me strength (Philippians 4:13).

It is in Your will, not my will, that I pray these prayers. I know my way is stupid; but God, Your way brings forgiveness, power, courage, boldness, healing, redemption, hope, love, and peace. I choose Your way! In Jesus' mighty and powerful name, I pray, Amen!

Acknowledgements

Sorbe

I have met many people along this journey with Johnson. But no better friends could have been found than the ones that I found in Wisconsin. Those dearest to me, you know who you are. We will be friends to the end and into eternity.

To my mother who without her Christ-like determination to see to it that my eyes stayed heaven bound during trials, I might have missed seeing Jesus holding me through them all.

To my father, without whom my perspective on life would have been dull. Thank you for your positive (and often humorous) influence on my life.

A huge thank you to the women who were a part of the Stupid book studies, both in MN and WI, allowing Johnson and I a safe space to pre-screen what the Lord had put on our hearts for this book. Without your input and encouragement, we may not have had the courage to send it to the publishers.

Thank you to both Jessi and Heather whose expertise in grammar, sentence structure, tense continuity (where I struggled the most), and the many questions they answered and the endless time they took during this endeavor to step in with us to make this book flow like it should. What a blessing you both were and my gratitude is deep and wide.

What a blessing this journey has been. I am ready to step into the next adventure. Take the reins, Lord, it's all about you!

Johnson

Written thank you's have always been a challenge for me. How do you convey in just a few sentences the depth of gratitude and love you have for people who have sacrificed so much for you. Jesus, please reveal my heart to each of these incredible people you put in my life.

Mark Johnson, I am grateful for you, my gentle protector! Thank you for supporting me in writing and in sharing our story. I love you; I like you. I have cried tears of gratitude to Jesus that you are still on this Earth with me. The Lord brought these verses to mind concerning your testimony. 2 Corinthians 1:8-10, "I think you ought to know, dear brothers, about the hard time we went through in Asia. We were really crushed and overwhelmed and feared we would never live through it. We felt we were doomed to die and saw how powerless we were to help ourselves; but that was good, for then we put everything into the hands of God, who alone could save us, for he can even raise the dead. And he did help us and saved us from a terrible death; yes, and we expect him to do it again and again."

Thank you to our children: Angela, Zoey, Lydia, Caelyn, Felicity, and Enoch. You have each taught me so much about genuine, deep, and powerful faith in Christ. Being your mom is a privilege and gift! It makes my heart burst with joy every time you join me on adventures with Jesus!

Mom! Dad! I love you. This book wouldn't have been possible without your support! You cared for my children to give me time to work on this project and space to recover during all of Mark's health crises'. Your support and love are mind blowing. Thank you!

Alan, Kathy, and Kim, thank-you for the excellent care you took of Mark while he was recovering from his knee surgery. I love you! I was able to focus on my children and writing because I knew you were taking care of him! You are wonderful!

Heather, Ryan, Jesse, Nate, Hannah, Lisa, Joe, and Tony, your help with editing, revising, and talking through the best way to correctly convey my thoughts. It was such a blessing to get to know each of you better through this process! You have all become family and I love you.

Notes

Bible Translations

This book is littered with scripture! As you read through it, you'll discover great intentionality here! You'll also notice we use MANY Bible translations and you may find yourself wondering "Why?".

What is the purpose of utilizing multiple Bible translations? Whether you are a seasoned Christ-follower or just beginning your walk with the Lord, this is not an uncommon question. Many people find themselves drawn to certain translations and will often stick with just the one. This is not an inherently bad thing. The Word of God is just that... His Word. Scripture is Scripture.

The usefulness of utilizing different translations comes into play when you consider how the Bible has been translated. While some translations are more literal, others are more "thought for thought." Reading scripture from both perspectives can allow you to grasp the meaning of the text in new ways. Sometimes, looking at the same verse in multiple translations will lead you to what we call an "Aha!" moment.

We pray whichever "version" you read, His Word comes alive as you dive into scripture and incorporate it into your daily life!

AMP–Amplified Bible. The Lockman Foundation, 2015. https://www.biblegateway.com/versions/Amplified-Bible-AMP/

AMPC–Amplified Bible, Classic Edition. The Lockman Foundation, 1965. https://www.biblegateway.com/versions/Amplified-Bible-Classic-Edition-AMPC

BSB–The Holy Bible: Berean Study Bible. Bible Hub, 2020. https://berean.bible/

ESV–English Standard Version Bible. Crossway, 2011. https://www.esv.org/

KJ2000–Holy Bible: King James 2000. Dr. Robert A. Couric, 1999. https://www.kingjames2000.com/

KJV–The Holy Bible, King James Version. Cambridge Edition: 1769; King James Bible Online, 2022. www.kingjamesbibleonline.org.

NASB–New American Standard Bible. The Lockman Foundation, 2020. https://www.biblegateway.com/versions/New-American-Standard-Bible-NASB/

NKJV–New King James Version. Thomas Nelson, 1982. https://www.biblegateway.com/versions/New-King-James-Version-NKJV-Bible/

NIV–New International Version. Biblica, 2011. Bible Gateway, www.biblegateway.com/versions/NewInternational-Version-NIV-Bible/

NLT–Holy Bible: New Living Translation. Wheaton, Ill: Tyndale House Publishers, 2004. Print.

NMV–New Messianic Version Bible. TovRose, 2012. https://www.bible.com/en-GB/versions/2135-nmv-new-messianic-version-bible

MSG–The Message: The Bible in Contemporary Language. Peterson, Eugene H. Colorado Springs: NavPress, 2002. Print.

TLB–The Living Bible, Tyndale House Publishers, 1971, https://www.biblegateway.com/versions/The-Living-Bible-TLB/

TPT–The Passion Translation. Passion & Fire Ministries, Inc. 2020. https://www.thepassiontranslation.com/

References

OPEN

1. "Open." *Merriam-Webster.com.* Merriam-Webster, 2022. Web. 21 January 2022.

Chapter 3: Start With Open

1. http://www.womenhorseshealing.com; Nancy Gustafson & Kelly Heller
2. Sheets, Dutch. "Chapter 3: Listen Slowly." *Watchman Prayer: Keeping the Enemy out While Protecting Your Family, Home, and Community*, Regal, Ventura, CA, 2008, p. 44.
3. Jeremiah 29:13
4. Jeremiah 29:11
5. Deuteronomy 34:7
6. "Open." *Merriam-Webster.com.* Merriam-Webster, 2022. Web. 21 January 2022.
7. Speaking our prayers out loud... There is something very powerful and moving in the spiritual realm when we speak things out loud. It is a declaration into our lives or our situation. It causes us to focus on what we are saying. It is a door to vulnerability that can be hard for many of us and this is precisely why it is so powerful. Consider when you say, "I love you." Just thinking "I love you" doesn't negate the truth and validity of your love; when you say it out loud you

are making a proclamation. It brings the love you feel into existence in that space where you've just spoken. It's powerful and moving. Trust me in this; speak these prayers out loud. (John 6:63, Hebrews 4:12)

8. Forgiving is essential to your breakthrough! You may be asking, how can I ever forgive this person for what they've done to me?! Forgiveness is a weapon of God's (Ephesians 4:31-32, Hebrews 12:14-15). Just like the joy of the Lord is our strength, truth brings freedom, love covers a multitude of sins and is a heap of burning coals on your enemy's head...Forgiveness is a powerful tool that the enemy cannot win against! Forgiveness releases the enemy's hold over you. You see, when someone does something to hurt you, the enemy will use that inflicted pain to torment you day and night. This tactic of the enemy allows that person to continue to hurt you over and over and over. While they may have moved on with their lives, you are stuck dealing with it. Unfair, right? It is unfair; and, that's exactly how the devil fights...unfairly! So we are going to use a weapon in our arsenal, which comes from God, against the devil in order to untether his strongholds of torment over us. In obedience, I ask that you say this prayer out loud, entering into the memory the Holy Spirit brought to your mind earlier. We are going to remove ALL of satan's power and authority over you in that memory and allow the Holy Spirit to heal your heart from the pain inflicted upon you! (Matthew 6:14-15, James 4:7, 1 John 1:9, Ephesians 4:27, Psalms 103:3, Romans 12:1-2, Luke 4:18-19, Hebrews 9:14, John 14:26)

<u>Chapter 4: Be Open</u>

1. Sheets, Dutch. "Chapter 1: Looking For A Few Good Watchmen " *Watchman Prayer: Keeping the Enemy out While*

Protecting Your Family, Home, and Community, Regal, Ventura, CA, 2008, p. 19.
2. Isaiah 52-53.

Chapter 5: Fully Open

1. "Control." *Merriam-Webster.com.* Merriam-Webster, 2022. Web. 21 January 2022.
2. Philippians 4:6-7.
3. Lewis, C. S.. The Case for Christianity. United States, Simon & Schuster, 1999.
4. "Defend Young Minds™: Kids Can Learn to Reject Pornography." *Defend Young Minds™ | Kids Can Learn to Reject Pornography*. Jenson, Kristen A. "Good Pictures Bad Pictures: Books: Defend Young Minds, 1 Oct. 2018, http://www.defendyoungminds.com/product/good-pictures-bad-pictures.
5. Deuteronomy 17:14.
6. Russel, D. S. *Between the Testaments*, Fortress Press, Minneapolis, MN, 1960.

Chapter 6: Trust–He Is Good (Active Not Passive)

1. James 1:2-3, Romans 8:28.
2. Ephesians 6:16.
3. Habakkuk 1-3.
4. Hebrews 4:1, Hebrews 4:10-11, Genesis 2:2-3.
5. "Trust." *Merriam-Webster.com.* Merriam-Webster, 2022. Web. 21 January 2022.

Chapter 7: Suck It Up and Drive On

1. Romans 7:14-25 (MSG).

2. Mosley, Seth. Smallbone, Joel. Smallbone, Luke. "Fix My Eyes." *Run WIld. Live Free. Love Strong.* Celi Mosley. 2014. CD.
3. Romans 5:3-10.

Chapter 8: Permission to Ask Questions

1. We encourage you to look into a few different communication resources! There are several great "tests" out there to help you discover more about your own personality, how God designed you, and the ways in which you best communicate with others. Tests like the Enneagram provide interesting insight into why we respond the way we do in varying situations. We would also recommend checking out a few books like "Keep Your Love On" by Danny Silk or "The Five Love Languages" by Gary Chapman.

Chapter 9: Killing Fear

1. Luke 10:19.
2. Luke 10:18.
3. John 16:7.
4. Luke 10:18.
5. Genesis 1:27.
6. 2 Cor 5:17.
7. James 4:7-8, I Thes 5:16-18, I Peter 4:8, 2 Chron 20:1-25, 2 Cor 2:5-11.
8. Titus 1:2, Hebrews 6:18, John 8:44.
9. "Belief." *Merriam-Webster.com.* Merriam-Webster, 2022. Web. 21 January 2022.
10. Guttman, A. "Advertising spending in the U.S. 2015-2022." Statista. Mar 28, 2019. Web. 21 January 2022.
11. 1 Chron 29:15, 1 Peter 2:11, Hebrews 11:13.

12. John 15:19, John 17:14-16, John 3:16, Romans 12:1-2, Col 3:2, 1 John 2:15-19, James 4:4, Philippians 3:20-21, Ephesians 6:12, Matthew 7:16-20, Revelation 21:1-27.
13. John 1:14a; See, also, Romans 8:3, Gal 4:4-5, Phil 2:6-8, John 5:19, John 5:30, John 8:28).
14. Philippians 2:8.
15. Matthew 8:28-34.
16. Mark 8:37.
17. Luther, Martin. "How Martin Luther Dealt With the Devil" *Issues, Etc. Journal. Vol. 2 No. 2.* Don Matzat. December 1996.

Chapter 10: Passivity is for Losers

1. 1 John 4:4.
2. 2 Corinthians 3:18.
3. Colossians 2:10.
4. Hebrews 10:15-25.
5. 2 Corinthians 5:17, Romans 6.

Chapter 11: Death Blow–Know Your Identity

1. Judges 6:13.
2. Judges 6:14.
3. Judges 6:15.
4. Judges 6:16.
5. Judges 6:36-40.
6. Judges 7:2.
7. Judges 7:12.
8. Judges 7:13.
9. Philippians 4:13.
10. 1 Corinthians 2:12
11. 1 Corinthians 2:16

About Jen Johnson

Jen is a freckled faced, red headed, drama nerd, who loves to encourage and make people laugh. She is passionate about prayer and walking hurting people through redeeming memories. Jen is the author of, *The House of Envy*, which is the first of her Christian allegorical trilogy from the Dark Mountain Series. Book 2, *The Coliseum of Power*, set to release in the winter of 2022.

Jen is married to Mark and together they have six children. Three years ago Mark and Jen were in a car accident that left Mark with Brain damage requiring him to live away from his family in order to recover.

During this very difficult season, Jen and Jenn Ministries was born and they co-authored this book.

"I believe that God is in the business of healing deep emotional wounds. His way is vastly superior to anything I can do, and He is good."
~Jen

About Jenn Sorbe

Jenn is a powerful speaker with a heart for intercession. Being a prior service military soldier, she has a unique perspective of Spiritual Warfare that has opened up a platform to speak to both men and women. With stories from her own life, Jenn brings humor into tough subjects that many find relatable. She is a lover of the Bible and Biblical teachings that show us that God uses unqualified people to great and mighty things in the Kingdom. When you listen to Jenn, you can expect to feel the urge to grab your spiritual sword and shield and step into fighting the war between good and evil. She is married to Brian. Together they have 4 children.

Decide/Choose to TRUST in the Lord with ALL your heart
and lean NOT UNTO your OWN understanding.

But

in ALL your ways, submit it all (yes, all. Open those hands
and give it) to the Holy Spirit {Christ}. And if you do...
He WILL make that path of yours straight.

#OPEN #TRUSTTHEPROCESS #NOFEAR

Adapted from my life verse in Proverbs 3
that my mother used to sing to me.
~Jenn

CPSIA information can be obtained
at www.ICGtesting.com
Printed in the USA
LVHW020020081122
732513LV00007B/88

9 781662 853951